INTERMEDIATE

The Complete Mandolin Method

Beginning · Intermediate · Mastering

GREG HORNE

Alfred Music Publishing Co., Inc.
P.O. Box 10003
Van Nuys, CA 91410-0003
alfred.com

ISBN-10: 0-7390-3472-3 (Book & CD)
ISBN-13: 978-0-7390-3472-9 (Book & CD)

CD recorded at Grinning Deer Studios, Knoxville, TN
Cover photograph: Karen Miller
Thanks to Sound To Earth, Ltd for use of the Weber Fern mandolin on the cover
and other Weber models for the interior photographs in this book.

TABLE OF CONTENTS

Track 1

A compact disc is included with each book of this series. Using these discs will help make learning more enjoyable and the information more meaningful. The CD will help you play the correct notes, rhythms and feel of each example. The track numbers below the symbols correspond directly to the example you want to hear. Have fun!

ABOUT THE AUTHOR

PHOTO • JOHN BLACK

Greg Horne is a performer, writer, producer and teacher. He holds a Bachelor of Arts in Music from the College of Wooster, and pursued graduate studies at the University of Mississippi's Center for the Study of Southern Culture. Greg was an instructor at the National Guitar Workshop's summer campuses from 1990 to 2011, specializing in songwriting and acoustic courses. He is the author of *The Complete Acoustic Guitar Method*, and co-author of *The Multi-Instrumental Guitarist*, also published by Alfred Music Publishing. Greg has produced several albums of his own songs, as well as producing and performing on projects for other artists. He lives in Knoxville, Tennessee. For more information or to contact Greg, visit www.greghornemusic.com.

Greg Horne plays Weber Mandolins made by Sound To Earth, Ltd in Belgrade, Montana (www.soundtoearth.com). They are heard on the CD that accompanies this book.

Greg Horne sends his special thanks to Paula Jean Lewis and Bruce Weber of Sound To Earth, David Lovett, Tim Worman, Pick'n'Grin (www.pickngrin.com), Nat Gunod, Wayne Fugate and his students.

INTRODUCTION

Welcome to *Intermediate Mandolin*, the second volume in the *Complete Mandolin Method*. This book picks up directly from the skills and tunes you learned in *Beginning Mandolin*. Here you will expand those skills, build your repertoire and solidify your foundation in music theory and improvisation.

WHO SHOULD USE THIS BOOK

While this book can be of benefit to players at all stages, it does assume that you know some of the basics that are covered in *Beginning Mandolin*. In order to get the most out of this book, you should be comfortable with the following techniques and skills:

- The names of the open strings and the structure of the music alphabet (also called the chromatic scale)
- Alternate (or "down-up") picking
- The basic structure and fingering of a major scale
- Strumming a steady beat using open chords
- Moveable chords (chords with no open strings) and finding new chords on the neck using moveable shapes
- Playing chords and improvising a simple lead on a 12-bar blues

DO I HAVE TO READ MUSIC/WILL I LEARN TO READ MUSIC?

You do not have to read music to use this book, all examples include TAB or chord graphs. However, a basic knowledge of pitch and rhythm notation (see pages 6–7) will help you learn the examples in this book more accurately. This book does not teach you to read music without TAB. *Beginning Mandolin* covers this in a clear, step-by-step chapter.

WHAT'S IN THIS BOOK?

- Technique and skill development for more fluid picking and fingering
- Repertoire building using fiddle tunes, bluegrass standards and the blues
- Extensive improvisation and soloing using scales, chords, theory and practical applications
- New styles and techniques from jazz, Celtic, funk and Brazilian music
- Theory and knowledge of the fretboard covering the major scale, natural minor scale, pentatonic scales, triad chords, 7th chords, arpeggios and blues scales

HOW TO USE THIS BOOK

This book is arranged in individual lessons grouped into chapters by topic. You can work from the beginning to the end of the book, or skip around and work on a couple of chapters at a time. Each chapter is progressive, meaning each lesson within a chapter builds on the previous lesson.

WHERE DO I GO FROM HERE?

Intermediate Mandolin is designed to give you the basic foundation you need to go to jams and festivals, play in groups, and most of all to play for your own enjoyment. This book progresses directly to the third volume of the series, *Mastering Mandolin*, where you will further refine your skills and deepen your knowledge.

CHAPTER 1

Review: Reading Music

This book assumes that you have either completed *Beginning Mandolin,* or you consider yourself an intermediate player because of what you have learned from a teacher or on your own. While you don't have to read music to use this book, it will definitely help if you can. This section is included as a quick review or introduction to reading standard music notation and tablature (TAB). For a more thorough treatment of the subject, pick up *Beginning Mandolin.*

STAFF

Music is written on a *staff* containing five lines and four spaces. *Notes* are written on the lines and spaces, which are assigned letter names from the musical alphabet: A-B-C-D-E-F-G-A-B-C, etc.

CLEF

The *clef* indicates which note names coincide with a particular line or space. Different clefs are used for different instruments. Mandolin music is written in *G clef.* The inside curl of the G clef encircles the line which is called "G." When the G clef is placed on the second line, as in mandolin music, it is called the *treble clef.*

G clef

Using the G clef, the notes on the staff are as follows:

LEDGER LINES

Ledger lines are used to indicate pitches above and below the staff.

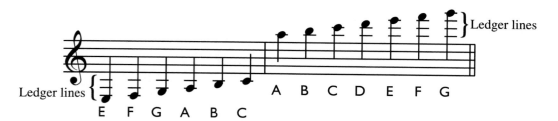

LESSON 2: TIME

The staff is divided by vertical lines called *bar lines*. The space between two bar lines is a *measure*. Each measure (or *bar*) is an equal unit of time. *Double bar lines* mark the end of a section or example.

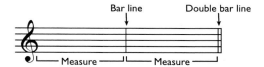

TIME SIGNATURE

Every piece of music has numbers at the beginning that tell you how to count the time.

Examples: $\frac{4}{4}$ $\frac{3}{4}$ $\frac{6}{8}$

The top number represents the number of beats, or counts, per measure.
The bottom number represents the type of note receiving one count.

   For example:

      When the bottom number is 4, the quarter note (see below) gets one count.

      When the bottom number is 8, the eighth note (see below) gets one count.

Sometimes a **C** is written in place of $\frac{4}{4}$ time. This is called *common time*.

NOTE AND REST VALUES IN $\frac{4}{4}$ TIME

These symbols indicate rhythm:

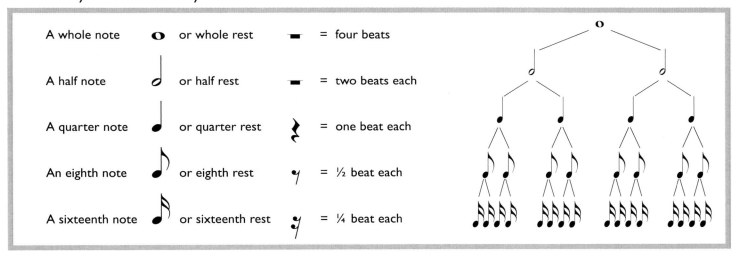

A whole note ● or whole rest ▬	= four beats
A half note ♩ or half rest ▬	= two beats each
A quarter note ♩ or quarter rest 𝄽	= one beat each
An eighth note ♪ or eighth rest	= ½ beat each
A sixteenth note ♬ or sixteenth rest	= ¼ beat each

Notes shorter than a quarter note are usually beamed together in groups:

LESSON 3: TABLATURE

Tablature (TAB) is a graphic representation of the strings of the mandolin. The top horizontal line represents the 1st string; the bottom line represents the 4th string. The numbers on the lines indicate which frets to play. The numbers below indicate left hand fingers.

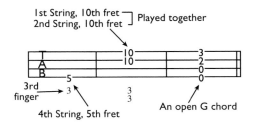

CHAPTER 2
Review: Scales and Chords

LESSON 1: MAJOR SCALES

In *Beginning Mandolin*, you learned to play the major scale in the keys of C, G, D and A. This book uses these keys extensively, especially in Chapter 4 (page 22). To review, remember that the major scale makes the familiar sound of "Do, Re, Mi, Fa, Sol, La, Ti, Do" (made famous in the movie *The Sound of Music*). The major scale is always constructed using the same formula of whole steps and half steps.

THE MAJOR SCALE FORMULA

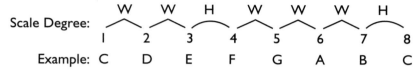

W = Whole step

H = Half step

Here are fingerings for the major scale in the keys of C, G, D and A in the open position of the mandolin. The *tonic* notes (scale degree number 1, the note the key is named for) have been highlighted.

C MAJOR SCALE

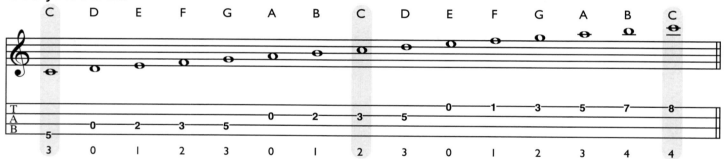

G MAJOR SCALE

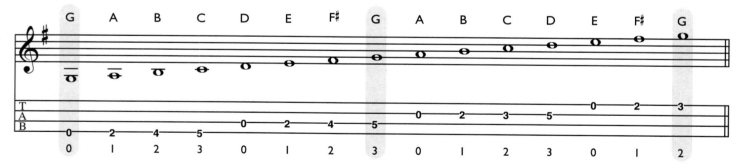

D MAJOR SCALE

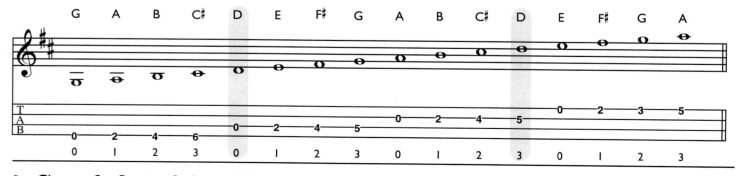

A MAJOR SCALE

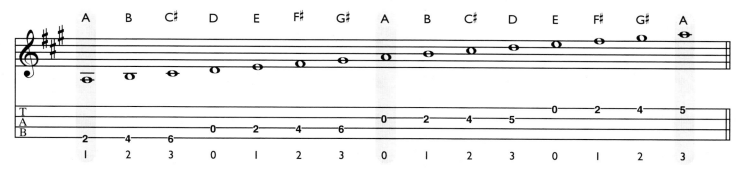

Below are many of the chord shapes you learned in *Beginning Mandolin*. These will be used throughout this book. Use this page as a reference for how to play these common chords. Some chords have many fingering possibilities. Unless the lesson gives you a specific fingering, you are free to experiment. New chords will also be introduced in later lessons.

Chords marked with an asterisk (*) are considered *moveable*. They can be moved up and down the neck to form chords in keys not shown here. For example, B7 can be moved one half step lower to form B♭7. All chords have the chord tones shown under the diagram (R=root, 3=3rd, 5=5th, 7=7th).

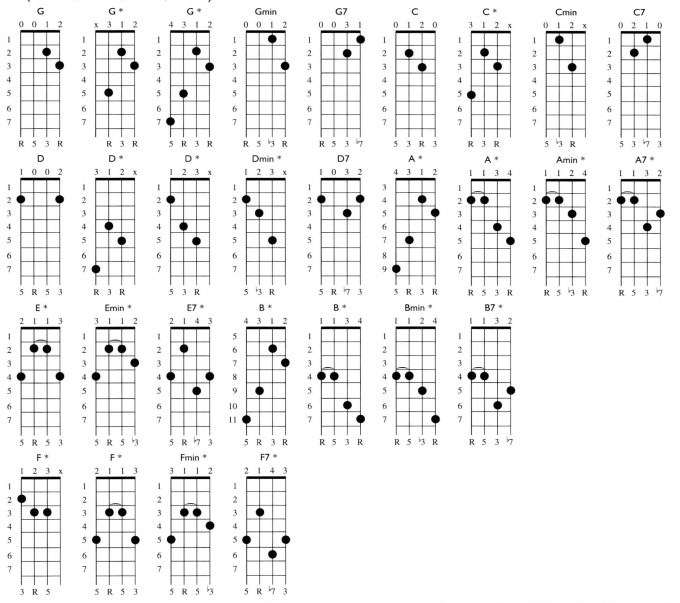

CHAPTER 3

Developing Technique

ACCURACY AND ECONOMY

Accuracy and economy of motion are the keys to building speed and agility in your playing. Try to identify the specific muscle movements required to play specific passages on the mandolin, and then eliminate any extra motion that detracts from your efficiency. Here are three crucial elements to improving your technique:

1. Be observant of your playing technique. Pay attention to how you hold the mandolin, your hand positions, your finger movements and your breathing.

2. Strive for economy of motion in your playing. Play with as little movement as possible and try to avoid tension. Stay loose and relaxed.

3. Practice exercises that address specific movements or techniques, and concentrate on the effects that the exercises were designed to achieve. Exercises have little effect if you simply try to play them as fast as possible.

Below are some exercises you can use to warm up your fingers and to build speed and accuracy. To get the maximum effect of these exercises, follow these pointers:

1. Concentrate on the motion of your fingers. Keep them "floating" close to the frets. Move them up and down like pistons in a car engine. *Don't play too fast!* It is better to play slowly and to focus on technical improvement than it is to concern yourself with simply being able to play fast.

2. Concentrate on synchronizing your picking hand with your fretting fingers. Feel the simultaneous forearm "twitch" that makes each note.

3. Practice these exercises for a few minutes at the beginning of each practice session. This will allow you to start off with the best technique possible. Soon the technique you develop in the exercises will start to show up in your regular playing.

The following exercises are shown on the 2nd string, but practice them on each string (using the same frets).

These exercises are written in $\frac{9}{8}$ and $\frac{6}{8}$. In $\frac{9}{8}$, there are nine eighth notes per bar, grouped in threes. This is called a *compound meter*, meaning that each beat is subdivided into three parts, resulting in a feeling of three beats per bar. $\frac{6}{8}$ feels like two beats per bar. This grouping is good for these exercises because it challenges you to keep track of your alternate picking, which must remain strict throughout! For more on compound meters and other picking patterns, see page 38. This issue is addressed again in *Mastering Mandolin*.

This one uses a major scale pattern that allows you to practice different finger spacings as you work up the neck. Try to play this with a *legato* touch, meaning the notes should be smoothly connected.

PISTON EXERCISE A: ASCENDING

Here's the same pattern coming down from the 12th fret. Try it on each string.

PISTON EXERCISE A: DESCENDING

Here's another one with notes grouped in threes to challenge your picking and give your 4th finger a workout.

PISTON EXERCISE B

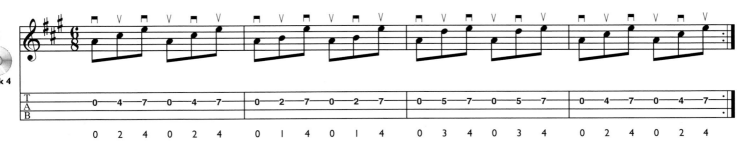

On page **46** of *Beginning Mandolin*, you learned the techniques of hammer-ons and pull-offs. To review, hammer-ons and pull-offs are the mandolinist's way of executing a *slur*. A slur is not what you do to your words after you've been to the dentist, but a term of musical expression. A slur connects two or more notes of different pitches so that the first one is articulated (played with the pick) and the others follow along without being picked.

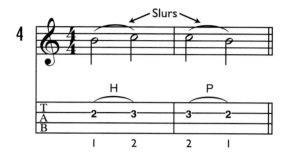

```
H = Hammer-on
P = Pull-off
```

It takes a bit of strength and a lot of accuracy to execute good hammer-ons and pull-offs on the mandolin. Here are a couple of tips:

HAMMER-ONS: Lift your finger directly over the note, then bring it down as if it was spring-loaded. Imagine that your finger is going to keep going on past the note and right through the neck. This is not so that you use more *force*, but so that you *follow through*. This will keep your finger from momentarily stopping at the string before it attempts to push the string to the fret.

PULL-OFFS: Remember to have both notes of the pull-off group pressed down before plucking. When pulling off, don't lift straight up. Instead, give a little sideways *snap* to the note. Some people snap their finger in toward the hand (a pulling motion), others push off of the note, away from the hand. Either way, this snapping motion will cause the note to sound much more clearly.

Try this exercise. It doesn't use every possible hammer-on or pull-off, but it gets most of them in there. Although there is no key signature, this exercise is written in A Major on the 2nd string. You could change it to A Minor by moving the 4th fret note (C♯) to the 3rd fret (C♮). Also try the same frets on other strings.

This exercise requires you to combine hammer-ons and pull-offs into triplets. It is shown in A Minor on the 2nd string, and D Major on the 3rd string. Practice both versions on every string.

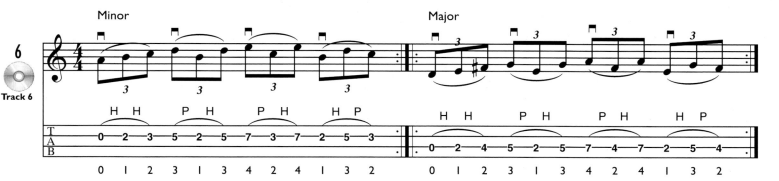

This one is a cool tag lick that could be used at the end of a solo. Try to pick each string only once!

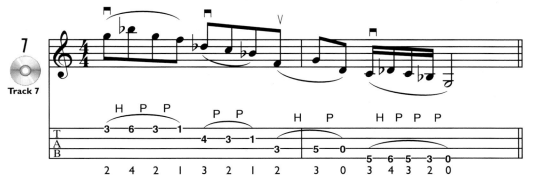

Tremolo (achieving sustain by rapidly repeating a note) is one of the most expressive characteristic sounds of the mandolin. It is also one of the most challenging. If you have worked through *Beginning Mandolin*, you have already experimented with tremolo.

TO MEASURE OR NOT TO MEASURE

In *Beginning Mandolin*, you learned about *unmeasured tremolo*. This means moving the pick down and up as rapidly as you can (or want to). Unmeasured tremolo allows you to change the speed and intensity of the effect at will. It is indicated in music by placing three slashes above or below the note head. Another kind of tremolo is *measured tremolo*. This means moving the pick to a specific division of the beat, often sixteenth notes. Sixteenth note measured tremolo is indicated with two slashes above or below the notehead.

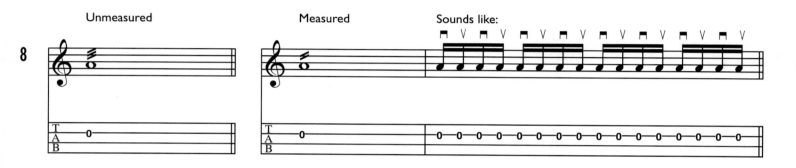

You can use measured tremolo to build and refine your technique. Try example 9, following these tips:

- Hold your arm and pick in a firm but relaxed grip, not the death grip used by the ancient warriors of the planet Voltron.

- Allow only the very point or tip of the pick to travel across the string.

- As you speed up, you will tighten up your muscles. This is natural. Stop often and relax. A little at a time, build up the length of time you can tremolo *and still stay relaxed!*

Track 8

TO PUNCTUATE OR NOT TO PUNCTUATE

Another aspect of fine-tuning your tremolo is punctuating the end of the note. Sometimes you will want to tremolo the entire duration of the note. Other times, you may want to stop the tremolo before the end of the note, allowing the note to decay naturally a bit before the next note. This punctuation generally occurs on a specific beat. The funny thing about punctuating tremolo is that it is very rarely notated in the music. It is generally left to the taste of the performer (that's you!)

One way to indicate the punctuation in music is to tie the tremoloed note to an untremoloed note, indicating where the tremolo should stop. The following tune incorporates this technique in a few spots, particularly the end of each repeated section.

This tune has a classical sound and challenges you to try tremolo with one string, two strings and four-string chords. Watch out for untremoloed notes and measured tremolos (only two slashes, indicating a sixteenth-note tremolo).

AIR ON THE SIDE OF CAUTION

Track 9

The mandolin's sound as a lead instrument in old-time and bluegrass music is heavily influenced by the fiddle. Mandolinists use *slides* as a way to imitate the more slippery, fretless sound of the fiddle. A slide is accomplished by gliding a finger along a string from one fret to another to create a smooth, sliding connection between the notes. Like hammer-ons and pull-offs, slides take a bit of practice. Spend some time working on slides with each finger on each string, ascending and descending. Keep in mind the following tips:

- As you slide, keep up the pressure on the string, so the sound continues.

- If the slide is only a distance of one fret (one half step), you can probably move just your finger without moving your whole hand position.

- If the slide is a distance of two frets (one whole step) or more, you should move your hand position with the slide. This will allow you to focus your strength on keeping the sliding finger in a good, firm fretting position while your hand and arm actually execute the slide.

Here's a cool blues lick that uses a slide for every finger.

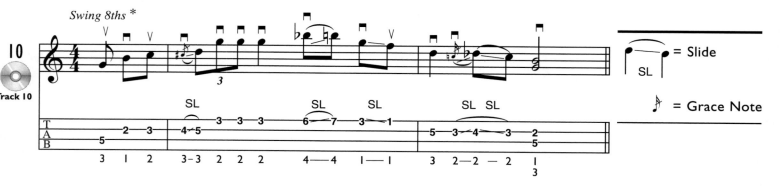

Note that slides may be articulated many ways. Here's a play-by-play of the lick in example 10.

1. The first slide in this lick is written with a *grace note* (a small note with a slash through it, played quickly, directly before the main note) connected with a dash (indicating the slide) and a slur. This means the slide will sound like a swoop up to the main note (D at the 5th fret of the 2nd string).

2. The second slide in this lick requires you to play an eighth note on B♭ (6th fret, 1st string), then slide it to B♮ (7th fret) without picking it (because of the slur marking). You should hear both notes distinctly and in rhythm.

3. The third slide connects a G (3rd fret) and an F (1st fret) on the 1st string, without a slur. You pick the G, slide down, and pick the F when you get there (no slur).

4. The fourth slide requires you to slide your 2nd finger from the 3rd fret (C) to the 4th (D♭) and back.

* Swing 8ths are discussed in *Beginning Mandolin*, page 54, and reviewed in this book on page 36.

UNISON SLIDES, DOUBLE-STOP SLIDES AND BEYOND

In *Beginning Mandolin* (page 42), you learned how *unison doubles* can add a fuller sound to notes played on the open E, A and D strings. For example, you can double an open E-note on the 1st string with the 7th fret of the 2nd string. To add even more zing to this effect, *slide into the fretted note* while picking the open note. Since you are sliding from the 5th fret to the 7th fret, you could use either your 4th finger or your 3rd finger. You will find situations that favor each one, so try it both ways!

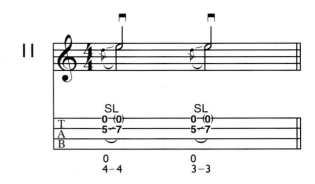

You can also slide *double stops* (two notes played at once). Just keep the pressure on, and keep your fingers firmly planted, allowing your hand and arm to do the work. Some players even like to slide three or four-note chords! This can be particularly cool (or sickly melodramatic, depending on your taste) when combined with tremolo.

Here's a little piece to try that incorporates all of the sliding techniques. Note that double-stop slides sometimes require you to end up in a slightly different finger placement from where you started! This happens in the slides in the last four bars.

SIGN SAYS "GONE NOODLING"

Track 11

Crosspicking is a technique used by mandolinists, guitarists and banjo players to create a sustaining, harp-like effect with melodies. In crosspicking, the individual notes of a melody are played on separate strings, allowing the decay of one note to overlap the start of the next. Crosspicking is also called *cross-string picking*.

Crosspicking was brought to the mandolin most dramatically by Jesse McReynolds of the famed bluegrass-brother duo, Jim and Jesse. Jesse wanted to imitate the three-finger banjo rolls he heard from players like Earl Scruggs. McReynolds' crosspicking style combines chords and rolls, scale runs and a peculiar picking pattern that makes an instantly recognizable, nearly unduplicatable sound.

You can develop your own style of crosspicking by finding ways to play melodies where the notes are played on separate strings. This takes some creative thinking, because often you have to use an open string or play a *lower* pitch on a *higher* string. To see how it works, here is a descending G *Major Pentatonic* scale (a five-note scale including the 1st, 2nd, 3rd, 5th and 6th degrees of the major scale, in this case, G, A, B, D and E) played first in open position, then using crosspicking.

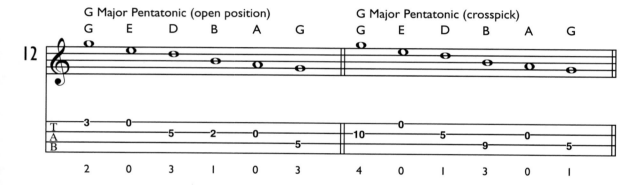

FINDING THE NOTES UP THE NECK

As you can see, crosspicking depends on an awareness of different spots on the neck to play the same note, so that you have choices for placement. There is a trick to it, though. Remember that each string tunes to the next lower adjacent string at the 7th fret. Therefore, the notes on the 2nd string, for example, from the 7th fret on, are the same as the notes on the 1st string, from the open string on. Chords also repeat up the neck in this way.

Here is an A Major scale in the first five frets, then starting on the 7th fret. Imagine that the 7th fret is a dividing line at which all open position scales and chords move one string lower. While these are not crosspicking fingerings, they illustrate how you can find new locations for notes and scales you already know.

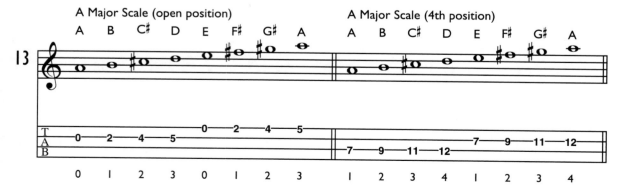

Here is the traditional fiddle tune "Turkey in the Straw" set in the key of G for crosspicking. In this tune, use alternate picking and watch all the fingerings very carefully! You may want to review the G Major scale (page 8). Chords are indicated above the music so that you use this opportunity to practice playing chords too. Chord fingerings may be found on page 9.

TURKEY IN THE STRAW (CROSSPICKING)

Track 12

A major feature of the Jesse McReynolds style is picking arpeggios (broken chords) in a *banjo-roll* style. Banjo rolls tend to group notes in threes. You can use two ways of picking to accomplish these rolls.

Strict Alternate Picking (Down-Up): Pick in the same strict down-up pattern you always use for eighth notes. This may cause you to make some interesting jumps from string to string with your pick, but it will keep your rhythm solid and will require less relearning for your hand.

Jesse McReynolds Roll Picking (Down-Up-Up): McReynolds uses a pattern in which he picks down on the lower string of a two- or three-string group, then up on the highest string, and up again on the adjacent lower string. While this can be very awkward at first, it can turn into a fluid motion that moves your hand in tiny circles, allowing you to build speed. This pattern is limited in its agility, however, and will often require you to break the pattern or turn it around backwards to get to the notes you want.

Here are two A chord rolls shown with both picking patterns.

A-Chord Roll No. 1

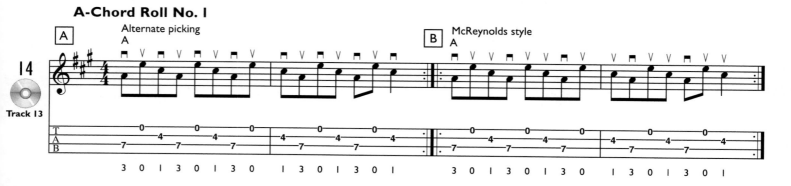

A-Chord Roll No. 2

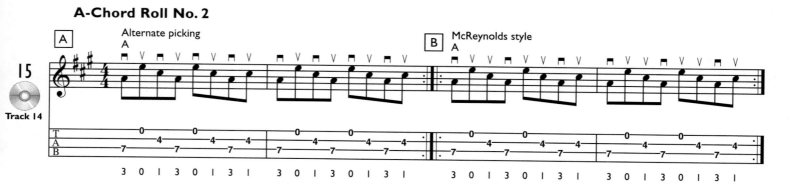

Here is a crosspicking tune based on the bluegrass standard "Lonesome Road Blues," also known as "Goin' Down the Road Feelin' Bad." This version is set in the key of A Major, and uses many chord shapes up the neck. Watch the fingerings carefully! The picking patterns are shown in the McReynolds style, but you should also try strict alternate picking to see which works better for you. It is a good idea to review the A Major scale on page 9. Chords are indicated above the music. Chord fingerings may also be found on page 9.

LONG LONESOME ROAD (CROSSPICKING)

Track 15

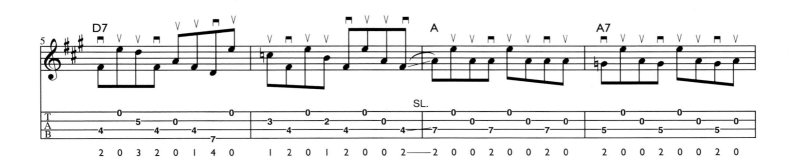

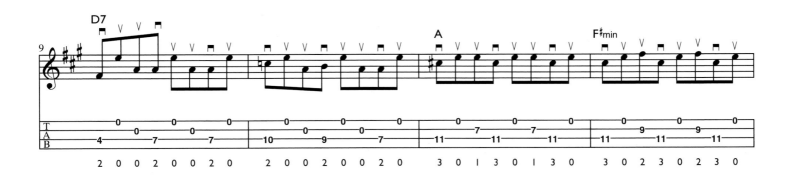

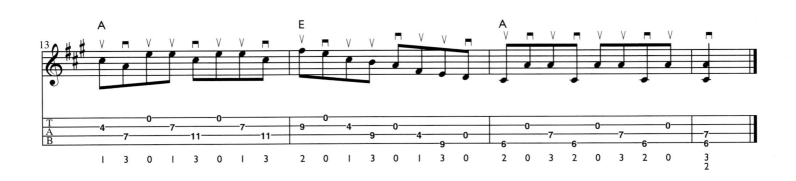

CHAPTER 4

Better Picking Through Fiddle Tunes

This chapter picks up from the fiddle tune techniques and tunes you learned in *Beginning Mandolin*. Because the mandolin's left-hand fingering is so similar to the fiddle, many of the moves and combinations heard in mandolin playing can be found in fiddle tunes. Learning fiddle tunes also builds a repertoire of music you can play at jams, parties, contests and gigs. The more tunes you learn, the faster you will be able to pick up new tunes on the fly.

The tunes in this chapter were chosen to illustrate moves and licks that come up in many tunes and solos. These licks are like *modules* that turn up in tune after tune. While there are hundreds of these modules in the tunes of the old-time, bluegrass and Celtic (British Isles) traditions, this chapter will introduce you to a very useful "starter set." These tunes are mostly from the Appalachian old-time tradition, but some come from the Celtic repertoire, and most cross over into bluegrass.

LESSON 1: HOW TO LEARN FOLK MUSIC

The music in this chapter is based on several folk music traditions. Folk music is considered an "oral tradition." This means that the method of learning was traditionally from the mouth of one person to the ears of another. With musical instruments, a better term might be an "aural tradition." In the days before mass media (most of the days of human history, in fact) an aspiring musician would sit at the feet of an elder player, watching and listening with the focus of a dog on a tennis ball, then run home and try to do the same thing.

Even now, there is no teacher of folk music like observing and playing music with other people who have mastered an instrument or style. There are nuances of sound and touch that are different from region to region, county to county and person to person. You will add your own stamp to the tradition when you play music with others.

HOW TO LEARN TUNES THE WRONG WAY

When you read music in a book, your instinct will be to try to play the whole tune, to "find out what happens next." As you reach a certain level of proficiency, you can indeed do this.

However, beginners often find that after they work on a tune long enough to figure it out, they are then "stuck" to the book. In other words, they have become proficient at reading the tune from the book, instead of playing the tune. When they encounter variations on the tune from other players, it can be confusing and frustrating. Remember, folk music and improvisational music like blues and jazz are fluid, living traditions. Everybody has a different version of a tune, but most of them will fit together one way or another!

HOW TO LEARN TUNES THE RIGHT WAY

Think about the goal of learning a tune: It may be to play with others, or just to have a new tune to play yourself. The important thing is to memorize the tune. You don't want to be dependent on your music books in a jam session. Folk music requires you to be flexible, quick to adapt and above all to have fun! If you know one or two tunes really well, you will have more fun than halfway knowing 20. As you go along, you may be able to pick up new songs by just hearing them. This is because you can hear the similarities and differences between the new tunes and those you already know.

Learn in Small Blocks and Get Away from the Written Music as Soon as Possible!
To take full advantage of the limited time you have to practice, try this technique when learning folk music:

1. **Get a general picture of the tune**. Look through the music to get an idea of the basic "shape" of the melody, as well as the structure of the tune. If you can, listen to the tune several times, both while looking at the music and without the music. Try to hum or sing along. The more the melody gets in your ear through singing, the easier it will be to know if you are playing it right. Old-timers call this process "setting the tune in your head."

2. **Work on just a small block of information at a time.** This may be as small as one move or one beat, or as much as a bar or phrase. Most folk music is made up of tiny melodic ideas and moves. Many of these little blocks or modules occur over and over again as you learn new songs. They just combine and recombine in different ways like atoms and molecules. Be aware that as you learn one tune, some of the same moves may appear in many other tunes. The hard work you do now will pay off tenfold!

3. **Start memorizing right away.** Play your tiny block over and over (and over and over) without looking at the music. Check back occasionally to make sure you've got it right, but then go back to playing it from memory.

4. **Work on the next block.** When you have it down, go back and attach it to the first block to make a bigger block. Think of those little plastic blocks kids play with: two small blocks stick together to make one big one. Pretty soon the kid's built a space city with a working monorail and sustainable power grid. And all you want to do is to play a 16-bar fiddle tune!

5. **Go back and play your old tunes often!** This is called *repertoire building*. You need to build your collection of tunes, then make sure they stay dusted off and road-worthy. You never know when you might need to jam "Cripple Creek" one more time.

This process may seem slow, but actually it is the fastest way to learn a tune. If you learn just one or two bars of music a day, you can learn a new tune every week. One year and you've got fifty tunes by heart (or five tunes on ten instruments, you pickin' fool, you), with two weeks off for summer bluegrass festivals.

GET OUT AND PLAY

Folk music is meant to be shared, like conversation, food and love. Don't be afraid to get out and play. Just pay attention to what other people are doing and try to match them, even if it's only for one session. Every tradition deserves respect. Good luck and remember to have fun!

In *Beginning Mandolin*, the fiddle tunes and bluegrass songs were written in $\frac{4}{4}$ time, counting four quarter notes to every measure. This is a good way to count when you are practicing slowly to learn a tune. When you get the tune up to speed, however, you may find that counting every beat will just wear out your foot from tapping, and may even slow you down.

Most old-time, Celtic, and bluegrass music is actually set in *cut time*. Cut time looks just like $\frac{4}{4}$ on the page except for the inclusion of the symbol for cut time (¢), but instead of tapping and counting all four beats, you tap on the half notes (every two beats). In other words, you have "cut" $\frac{4}{4}$ into $\frac{2}{2}$ (two half notes per measure). Here's what it looks like to your foot:

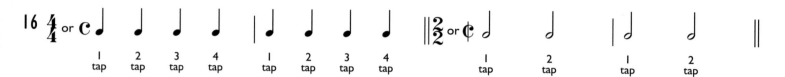

The fiddle tunes in this book will be shown in cut time. As you start learning them, you may want to count and tap all four beats at a slow speed. Then, as you speed up, just cut your number of foot taps in half.

MODULE NO. 1: THE "FIRE ON THE MOUNTAIN" LICK

This chapter will introduce you to many moves that are used to make up fiddle tunes and improvise *breaks* (solos). These moves do not actually have names or numbers, nor do they originate with any particular tune. The names and numbers given are just to help you as memory aids.

Here is a move that shows up in dozens of tunes, and gets a real workout in "Fire on the Mountain." This tune uses the lick in two keys, A Major and D Major. You may want to review these scales on pages 8 and 9. Try each of these variations on the move.

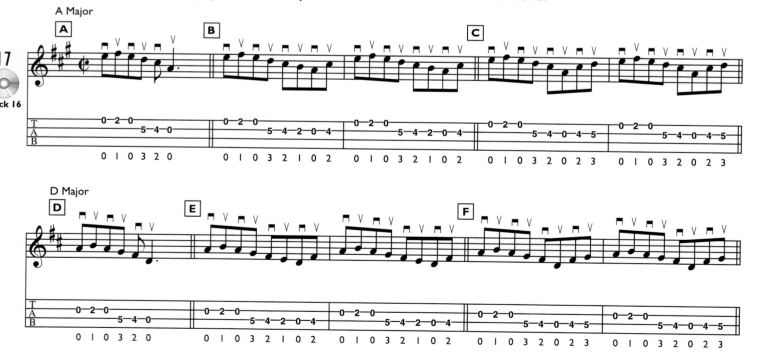

Now try the whole tune. Chords are indicated above the music, and fingerings may be found on page 9. You can find great versions of this tune from many bands, including Bill Monroe, the Stanley Brothers, the Highwoods String Band and others. The title is very common, however, and sometimes refers to other tunes or variants. Tracking down tunes is part of the fun of being a musician!

Many tunes you will learn have an A part and a B part that are equal in length, with each part repeated before moving on. This tune has a little extra part that extends the end of the B part (shown as the 2nd ending of the B part). Old-timers call tunes that have unequal A and B parts, extra beats, or unusual phrasing "crooked" or "uneven."

FIRE ON THE MOUNTAIN

Track 17

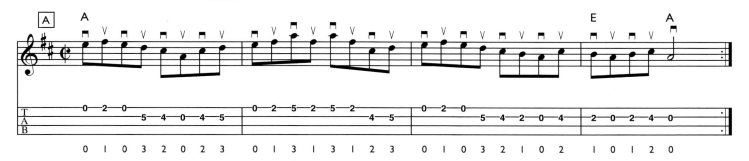

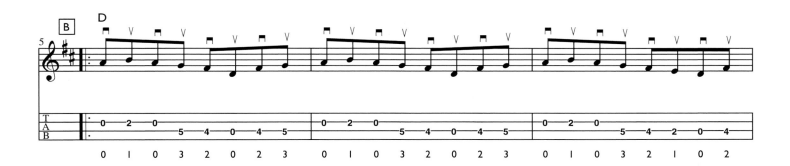

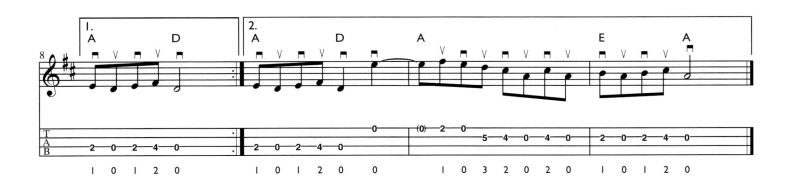

Sally Goodin was one of the first "hillbilly" songs recorded in the early 20th century. The performer was fiddler "Eck" Robertson, and his version represented what is known as *contest style*. In the contest style, a musician takes a traditional tune, often a hoedown or square dance tune, and creates many variations on the basic melody to demonstrate skill and virtuosity. Robertson's 1922 recording was so influential that musicians have been basing their versions on his variations ever since.

Part of the character of this tune is the way a few notes of the A Major scale (page 9) are used on the 2nd string at the start of the tune. In this version, based on "Eck" Robertson's, you get to combine and recombine ways of playing the A, B and C# notes in the open position of the 2nd string. You should work these out four notes (one big beat) at a time, then begin to string them together.

Here's "Sally Goodin" in a standard, two-part form. This is the basic tune upon which variations are built. Notice that in the 2nd and 3rd bar of the B part, the "Fire on the Mountain" lick from Lesson 2 makes an appearance. Chords are indicated above the music and fingerings may be found on page 9.

 ## SALLY GOODIN (STANDARD TWO-PART VERSION)
Track 18

On the next page are four variations that are used in contest versions of the tune. They sound good played in this order, but they can be shuffled around or recombined with the original A and B part of the tune. These variations are adapted from the fiddling of "Eck" Robertson, Kenny Baker, Ricky Skaggs and the mandolin of Bill Monroe.

Note that each variation should be repeated, and Variation No. 4 is twice as long as the others. Take it slow and steady. You'll be able to use the moves from this tune in lots of other solos and tunes soon!

SALLY GOODIN VARIATION NO. I

Track 19

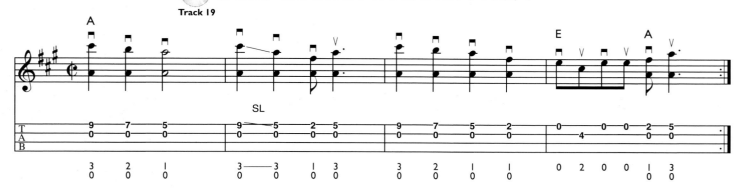

SALLY GOODIN VARIATION NO. 2

Track 20

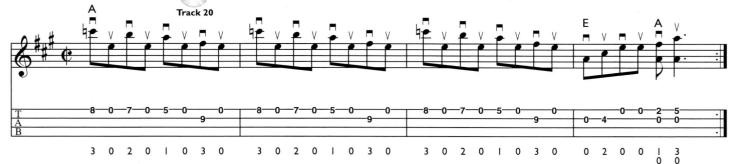

SALLY GOODIN VARIATION NO. 3

Track 21

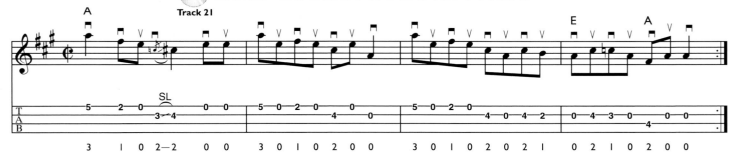

SALLY GOODIN VARIATION NO. 4

Track 22

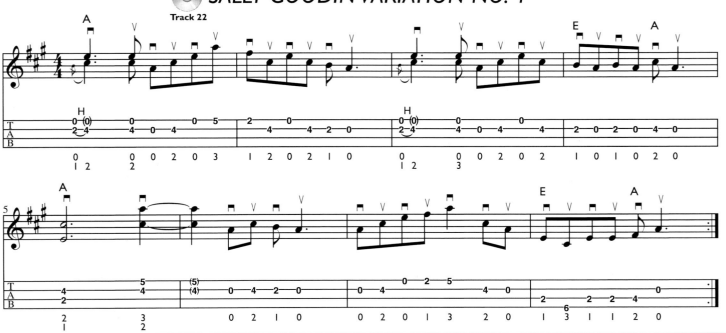

The last two lessons have mostly been in the key of A Major. "Kitchen Gal" on page 29 falls into the category of *modal tunes*, which are tunes that incorporate scales other than the major scale, often with a minor sound. Modal tunes generally have in common the lowered 3rd ($\flat$3) and lowered 7th ($\flat$7) scale degrees, but may have other variations to the scale as well.

"Kitchen Gal" uses two scales to make up its modal sound:

> A *Mixolydian mode*—Major scale with a $\flat$7, or G$\natural$ instead of G$\sharp$ in the key of A.
> A *Dorian mode*—Very much like a natural minor scale ($\flat$3, $\flat$6, $\flat$7, see page 70 of *Beginning Mandolin*) except 6 is not lowered, leaving a $\flat$3 and $\flat$7, or C and G in the key of A. Here are the two scales.

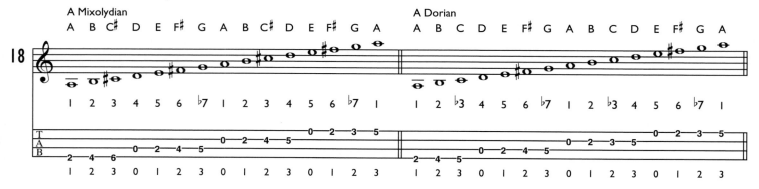

MODULE NO. 2 —THE SYNCOPATED FIDDLE SHUFFLE RHYTHM

On page 40 of *Beginning Mandolin*, you learned a basic picking rhythm based on the *shuffle* bowing pattern used by fiddlers. Here is that rhythm shown on an open E-note, followed by a new syncopated (emphasis shifted to the offbeats) variation you can use to jazz up your picking.

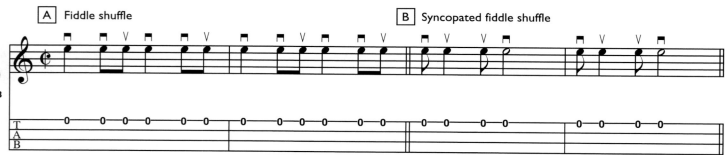

MODULE NO. 3 — THE "KITCHEN GAL" ENDING LICK

At the end of the B part of "Kitchen Gal," there is a small lick using part of the A Dorian scale. This lick turns up in variations in many modal, minor and Irish tunes. You will even see it later in this chapter in the key of G Major!

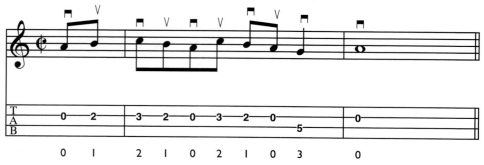

Now try "Kitchen Gal." Chords are indicated above the music and fingerings may be found on page 9. You will see several variants of the "Fire on the Mountain" lick, a syncopated fiddle shuffle and the A Dorian lick you just learned. Note that the A part is in A Mixolydian (using major A, G and E chords), while the B part is in A Dorian (using A Minor, G Major and E minor chords). This version is inspired by the fiddle of Alan Jabbour and the mandolin of Bertram Levy, both of the Hollow Rock String Band.

KITCHEN GAL

Track 25

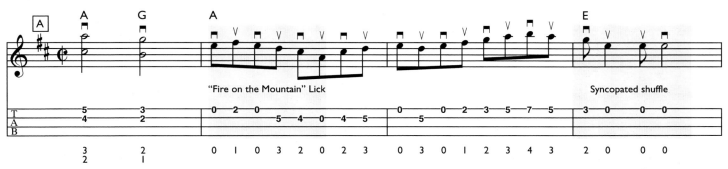

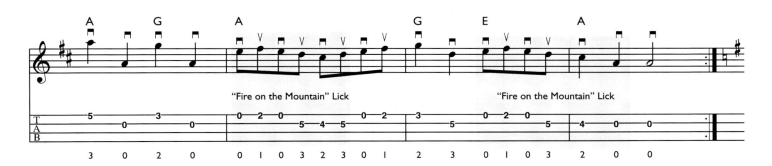

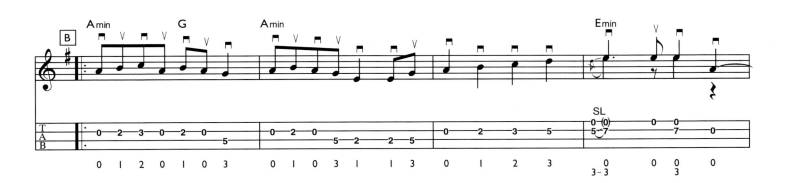

"Leather Britches" is another hoedown/square-dance/contest tune that has a minimalism and drive reminiscent of "Sally Goodin." It is in the key of G Major (page 8), allowing you to adapt some of what you have learned in A Major to this key. "Leather Britches" is thought to have descended from a Celtic tune called "Lord MacDonald's Reel," which does share many melodic passages in common with this tune.

"Leather Britches" has buried within it a couple of the moves you have already learned. For example, at the end of the first line, you will see a version of the "Fire on the Mountain" lick, moved down to the 3rd and 4th strings for the key of G.

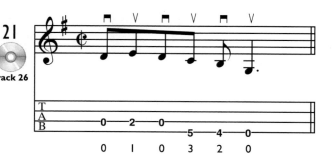

At the end of the A section, "Leather Britches" uses a move that is very similar to the end of "Kitchen Gal," except that it resolves to the key of G Major instead of A Dorian. Here are both passages for comparison.

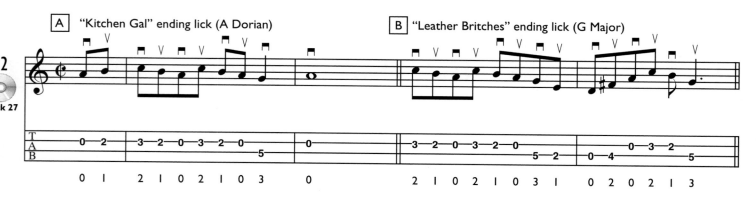

Now try the full "Leather Britches" on page 31. Chords are indicated above the music and fingerings may be found on page 9. Note that the B part is only half as long as the A part. Also included is a variation on the A part in a higher octave. If you use this variation, you should still follow it with the regular B part. This is indicated in the music with *D.S. al Fine* (*Del Segno al Fine*), which means "return to the sign 𝄋 and play until the *Fine*." Ordinarily, we would ignore repeat signs after having returned to the 𝄋 sign, but in this case one *should* take all of the repeats.

This version of "Leather Britches" is influenced by the fiddling of Vassar Clements.

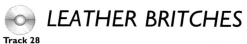

LEATHER BRITCHES

Track 28

Here's another tune in the key of G Major that will give you a break from the steady eighth notes you've been picking. "Seneca Square Dance" is another tune with many possible titles and relatives, including "Waiting on the Federals," "Georgia Boys," "Shoot That Turkey Buzzard" and "Davy Dugger," to name a few!

MODULE NO. 4 — THE SENECA SQUARE-DANCE-ENDING LICK

This lick appears at the end of both parts of this version of the tune. It also appears (moved one string higher) in many D Major tunes, including Lesson 7's "Johnny Don't Get Drunk." It provides a nice way to wrap up a phrase in a major key.

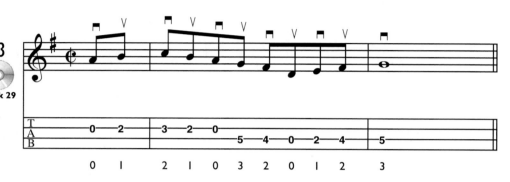

23

Track 29

PHOTO–MARK CARBONELLI/COURTESY OF SCOTT O'MALLEY & ASSOCIATES

__Norman Blake__ is famous for his proficiency on a variety of stringed instruments, including mandolin and acoustic guitar. He was one of the major bluegrass musicians of the 1970s, coming into prominence in the late 1960s, when he began appearing as a sideman with artists as diverse as June Carter and Bob Dylan. During the 1970s, he began a solo career that quickly became one of the most important and musically adventurous in the bluegrass style.

Now try the whole tune. Chords are indicated above the music and fingerings may be found on page 9. You will get a chance to use the ending lick on page 32 and the syncopated fiddle shuffle rhythm (page 28) a couple of times in the B part. This tune has a march-like sound that doesn't need to go too fast. This version is inspired by the 1927 recording by Fiddlin' Dave Neal, as well as John Hartford and Knoxville, Tennessee fiddler Tim Worman.

SENECA SQUARE DANCE

Track 30

This tune is in the key of D Major (page 8) but uses some moves from other tunes. The first one is Module No. 4 from "Seneca Square Dance." In "Johnny Don't Get Drunk," the lick is moved up one string for the key of D Major. Here are both versions.

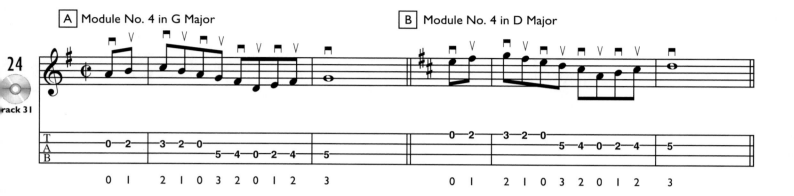

MODULE NO. 5 — THE I-V-I CADENCE LICK

A *cadence* is a melodic or harmonic statement at the end of a musical phrase which helps state the key of the tune. This little move first outlines the I chord of D Major (D), then the V chord (A) and then returns to I. The movement happens so quickly that it is often only heard in the melody and not in the accompanying chords. This is a good finger combination to work on for your fretting hand, and will also challenge your picking hand to move between strings on alternate strokes. If you look closely back at "Turkey in the Straw" on page 19, you will see this move transposed to G at the end of the A and B parts.

Here's the lick shown in D Major in both the high and low octaves.

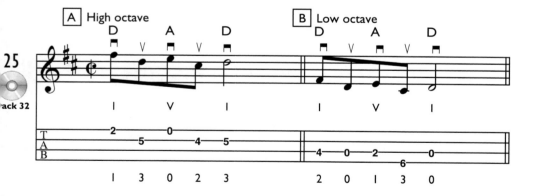

Now try the whole tune. Watch for syncopated rhythms and observe the picking indications.
Chords are indicated above the music and chord fingerings may be found on page 9.

Track 33

JOHNNY DON'T GET DRUNK

Ragtime tunes (called *rags*) are extremely fun to play on the mandolin. The classic ragtime instrument in the late 19th and early 20th century was the piano. Many piano tunes were adapted to string instruments, and new tunes were also composed by string players. Rags are characterized by very syncopated phrasing, more sophisticated harmony and multiple sections. The sharp attack of the mandolin string recalls the percussive sound of the piano, and makes the mandolin a perfect instrument for this music.

To get ready for this tune, review the C Major scale on page 8.

SWING 8THS—REVIEW

You learned about *Swing 8ths* in *Beginning Mandolin* (page 54). Many rags use the swing feel. To review, the underlying pulse of swing is a triplet feel. To get the feel of triplets, say this aloud to a steady beat: "trip-pul-let, trip-pul-let."

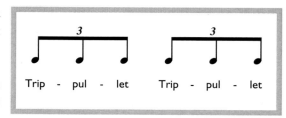

The *Swing 8ths* feel can be illustrated as a triplet with the first two notes tied together. In *Swing 8ths*, "1" is the first note of the triplet and the "&" is the last. In example 26, the *Swing 8ths* feel is shown in triplets and in regular eighth notes with the designation "*Swing 8ths.*" These two notations produce an identical rhythm.

MODULE NO. 6 — PICKING IN GROUPS OF THREE

The highly syncopated sound of ragtime is often a result of the grouping of notes in threes. These are not triplets, but instead normal eighth notes that are phrased in groups of threes. These phrases will challenge you to watch your alternate picking, as one group begins "down-up-down" and the next begins "up-down-up." Try the licks in example 27. They will reappear with harmony notes in the following tune.

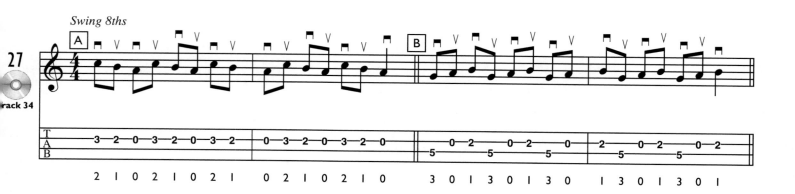

Here's a new tune written in the ragtime style. It pays tribute to the two most important influences on the construction of the modern American mandolin, Orville Gibson and Lloyd Loar. Most rags have three or more parts. This one is in two parts, but it includes a repeat of the A part at the end. This is designated by the marking *D.C. al Fine (Da Capo al Fine)*, which means to repeat from the top until you reach the point marked *Fine* (Italian for "song's over, clap now"). Chords are indicated above the music and chord fingerings may be found on page 9.

ORVILLE AND LLOYD'S RAG

Track 35

WORKING IN A COMPOUND METER

In this lesson you will cross the ocean to Ireland (unless you are already there) to explore the playing of *jigs*. A jig is a lively dance often based on a *compound meter*. The other tunes you have learned so far (except for a couple of short exercises on page 11) are in *simple meters*, where each beat is divided into two equal eighth notes. In a compound meter, the beat is divided into three equal eighth notes. The time signatures for compound meters usually have an 8 on the bottom. The top number, usually either a 6, 9 or 12, can be divided by 3 to produce the number of pulses (foot taps) in the measure.

The most common time signature for jigs is $\frac{6}{8}$. This time signature tells us that there are six eighth notes in every bar. Six divided by three gives us two big beats in each measure, with the dotted quarter note equaling one beat. In other words, $\frac{6}{8}$ is actually felt as two groups of three. You can count it either as "1–2–3–4–5–6," or more accurately, "1–&–ah, 2–&–ah." Try this counting and tapping exercise to get the idea. Stomp your foot loudly to make sure you get the feel of the two big beats that divide up the six small beats.

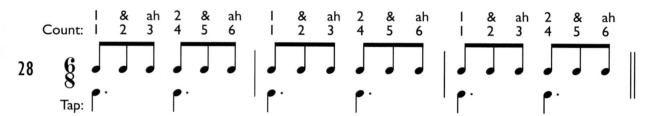

You may have realized by now that your pick can only move two directions (down and up, that is) and your beat now has three parts. How will you resolve this perplexing conundrum? Well, you could venture high into the Himalayas to seek the advice of a charming-yet-weatherbeaten guru, or you could try one of the following solutions.

$\frac{6}{8}$ PICKING SOLUTION NO. 1 (DOWN-UP-DOWN, DOWN-UP-DOWN)

This pattern is favored by the largest number of picked instrument players who play Celtic music. It allows you to feel the accent pattern of the two big beats, and brings that *accent* (louder note) pattern out in your tone naturally. It also makes it easy to transfer the technique to *slip jigs* in $\frac{9}{8}$. It takes a bit of practice to get the move going and keep the tempo even, so work slowly and be patient. Try this exercise on any open string.

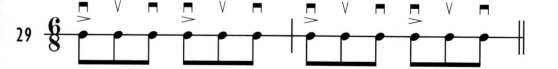

> = *Accent (Play louder)*

⁶⁄₈ PICKING SOLUTION NO. 2 (STRICT ALTERNATE PICKING)

This option adapts strict alternate picking (down-up-down-up-down-up) to the accent pattern felt in ⁶⁄₈ time. To practice it, you need to accent the downstroke on the first eighth note, and the upstroke on the 4th eighth note. Try this pattern on any open string.

The disadvantage of this pattern is that you have to keep the ⁶⁄₈ accent pattern in your head as it shifts under your picking. However, this pattern has the advantage of being consistent with the way you already play. It also has no limitations of speed, while the first pattern may reach its maximum velocity fairly quickly since it requires two consecutive downstrokes.

WHICH PICKING SOLUTION DO I USE?

In order to stay consistent with most mandolin teaching and materials, the remaining examples will be written using Pattern No. 1 (down-up-down, down-up-down). You could easily adapt the examples to alternate picking until you decide which is right for you.

RHYTHM PLAYING FOR JIGS

The simplest rhythm pattern is similar to the "boom, chick" beat heard in bluegrass.

Jig Strum Pattern No. 1

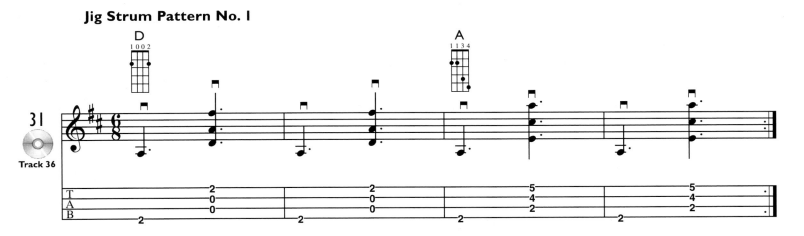

The next pattern uses constant eighth notes to create an insistent, galloping feel. Be sure to exaggerate the accents so that you can hear the compound meter clearly. Since all strings are strummed, no TAB is needed. Use the D and A chord fingerings shown in example 31.

Jig Strum Pattern No. 2

Here is a full-length jig to try in the key of D Major (page 8). As usual, you should work on this one bar, or even one beat at a time. This jig includes several arpeggios on D and A chords, which appear in many other tunes. It also ends each section on a G chord, which pulls you along to the next section, making you want to play it over again! Chords symbols are provided so that you can also practice your strumming. Use one of the strum patterns from page 39 (chord fingerings are shown on page 9).

MONEY IN BOTH POCKETS

Track 38

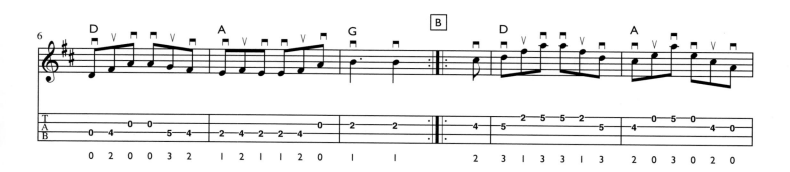

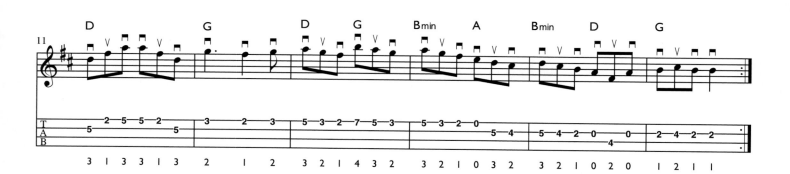

Here's another jig, this time in A Dorian (page 28). This jig has an addictive drive and a dark, bluesy sound. Musicians will often group tunes together into medleys. "D" tunes, for example, flow nicely into A Minor/modal tunes. "Scatter the Mud," for example, would make a good medley when preceded by "Money in Both Pockets." This version is inspired by the fiddling of Kevin Burke. Chords are indicated above the music and chord fingerings may be found on page 9.

SCATTER THE MUD

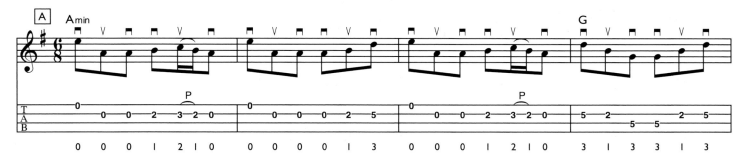

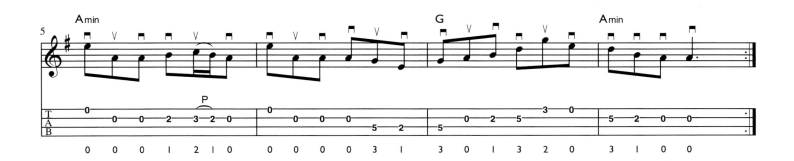

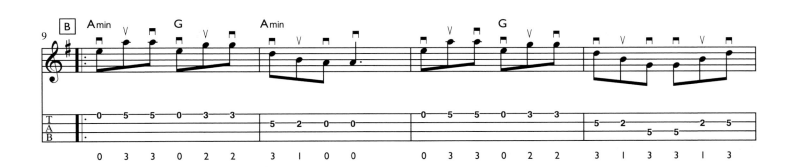

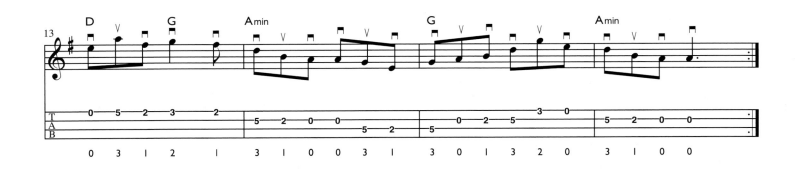

CHAPTER 5

Back to Bluegrass

RETURN OF THE CHOP

In *Beginning Mandolin* (page 61), you learned some basic bluegrass strumming built around the *chop*. The chop is the rhythmic backbone of bluegrass mandolin. Using moveable chords (with no open strings), you strum a backbeat rhythm—chopping on beats 2 and 4. Your left-hand fingers control the percussive effect by relaxing pressure just after (or sometimes during) the downstroke of the pick. Keep your right-hand and wrist loose and drop the weight of your hand across the strings with a flick of the wrist. If your wrist is tight or you try to use a "cranking" motion, your chop will sound stiff and harsh. Here's a review of the basic chop strum.

BASIC CHOP STRUM

Sometimes, you will want to very simply chop on beats 2 and 4 as shown above. If there is a bass player playing on beats 1 and 3, you will be able to "lock together" into a great groove. In order to feel the bluegrass groove better, many mandolinists will add a quiet downstroke on the 4th string on beats 1 and 3. This creates the "boom-chick-boom-chick" rhythm familiar in this kind of music. Here's the trick: play the "boom" note softly on beat 1 or 3, and hold your hand on the chord until you've "chopped" it on beat 2 or 4.

You can also add upstrokes to your strum. Now that your hand is moving in a steady beat throughout the measure, you can throw in an upstroke every now and then to syncopate the rhythm, making it move more. Try the pattern in example 34. The fingerings shown are typical of Bill Monroe's rhythm playing.

ADVANCED CHOP STRUM

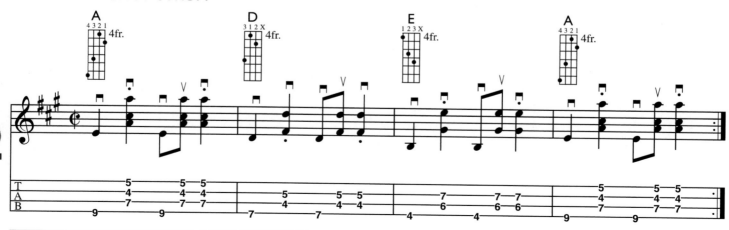

Here is a traditional song that will be used as the basis for this chapter. It was first recorded in 1927 by Dykes Magic City Trio, and has been a favorite ever since. The melody and structure are very close to many other bluegrass standards, especially "Rollin' In My Sweet Baby's Arms." "Free Little Bird" is originally in G Major, but has been set here in the key of A Major. Learn the melody and words, and for rhythm use the advanced chop strum with the chord fingerings from example 34 on page 42.

The performance on the CD available for this book includes a vocal performance of the song with an accompaniment.

FREE LITTLE BIRD
Track 42

In bluegrass, there are three basic roles that an instrumentalist may play at any given point in the song.

- **Lead:** Playing a solo break or you are the featured melody instrument.
- **Backup, or Rhythm:** Playing chords as part of the rhythm section.
- **Lead Backup:** This is an in-between state, where you are playing a more active form of backup that may include chords, tremolo and melodic fills around the vocal part or another soloist.

FILLS

A *fill* is a short melodic idea or lick that occurs during a space in the vocal part or instrumental melody. Playing fills is not like playing a full solo break. You must listen carefully to what is happening, so that your fills add spice to the main melody, without playing all over it. Fills occur when a vocal note is held at the end of a phrase, or during empty spaces in the phrasing.

Fills are generally improvised using blues licks, ideas from fiddle tunes and anything else you can think of. The more melodies you learn, the more you have to draw from to create fills and solos. Rhythmically, a fill will very often lead to a strong *chord tone* (a root, 3rd or 5th of the chord being played) on the downbeat (beat 1) of the upcoming bar. Think of a drum fill in rock or jazz—the drummer improvises something exciting in the last bar of a phrase, and punctuates it with a cymbal crash on the first beat of the new phrase.

Here is a sample lead backup arrangement of "Free Little Bird." Above the mandolin music and TAB are the melody and lyrics from page 43. This will help you see how the lead backup part sits under, and then fills the spaces in the melody. On the CD that is available for this book, you will hear this lead backup along with a vocal performance and simple backup. The second time through is just the vocal and simple backup so that you can create and practice playing your own lead backup part.

🔘 *FREE LITTLE BIRD—LEAD BACKUP*

Track 43

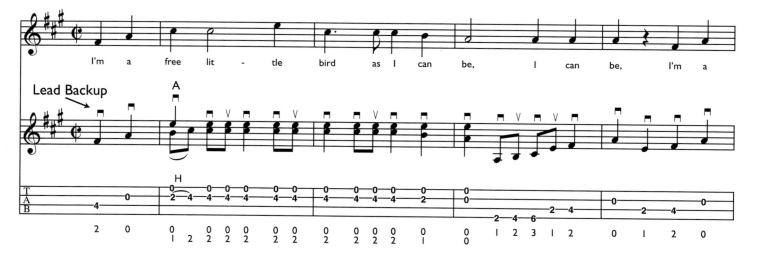

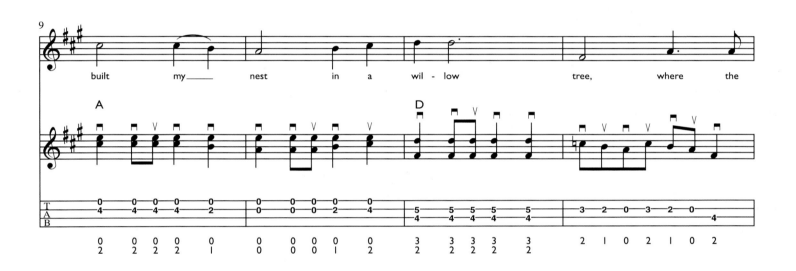

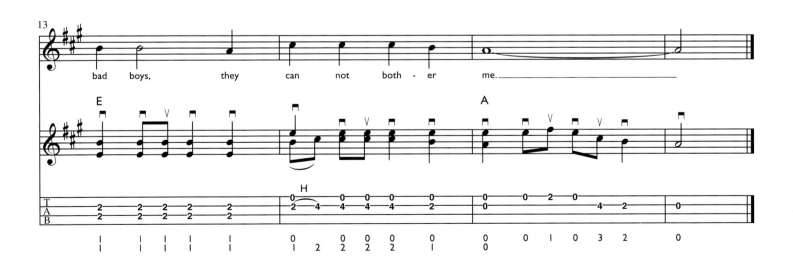

Bluegrass *breaks* (solos) are usually played over the verse and/or chorus of the tune itself. This allows you to take a couple of different approaches. On any given tune, you could play a *melodic break* or an *improvised break*.

A **melodic break** is based on the melody of the song. This may be the vocal melody or, in the case of an instrumental, the main tune.

An **improvised break** is based on the chord progression, but does not have to stick to the original melody. Lesson 4 (page 48) will cover improvised breaks.

TIPS FOR CONSTRUCTING MELODIC BREAKS

1. Learn a simple version of the melody of the song. This will give you a basic "skeleton" for your break. You can "flesh it out" with passing tones (page 38, *Beginning Mandolin*) between the main melody notes, and with harmony notes and fills.

2. Try imitating the voice with your mandolin. Sing the melody yourself, or work with a singer, and try to duplicate the rhythmic and melodic nuances you hear. This skill takes time to develop, so listen hard and be patient.

3. Though the melodic break is based on the melody, there are plenty of opportunities to improvise. You could syncopate rhythms, add blue notes (page 56, *Beginning Mandolin*) from the blues scale (♭3, ♭5 and ♭7, see fingering below), or improvise different passing tones.

4. Improvise or compose! Using the above tips, you can make up a new version of the melody on the spot. On the other hand, it is perfectly fine to work out specific breaks and practice them ahead of time so that you know what you're going to do when the man in the white hat turns around and says "Take it!"

Here is the A Blues scale. It incorporates the A Major scale (page 9) and the blue notes discussed above.

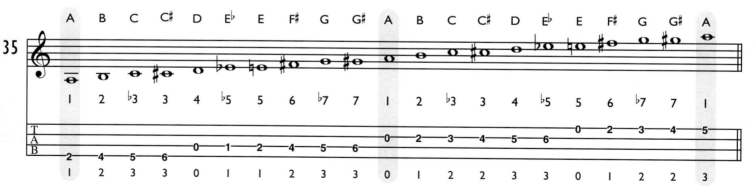

Here is a melodic break for "Free Little Bird." It incorporates hammer-ons, a unison slide (page 17), fiddle tune-style licks, tremolo (see page 14) and passing tones. There are also some blue notes. Remember the goal of a melodic break: even with all of the interesting things going on, you should still be able to hear the shape and structure of the main melody. It is as if the mandolin were "singing" the words of the song. On the CD that is available for this book, you will hear the break with chords, then the chord progression will repeat so you can try your own break.

FREE LITTLE BIRD—MELODIC BREAK

Track 44

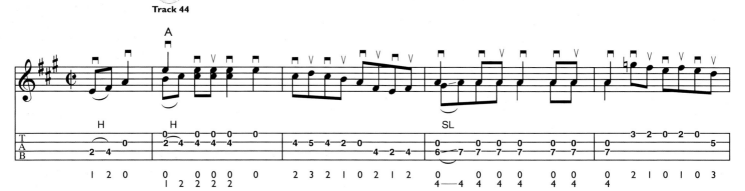

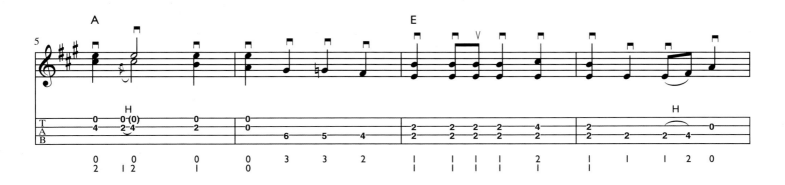

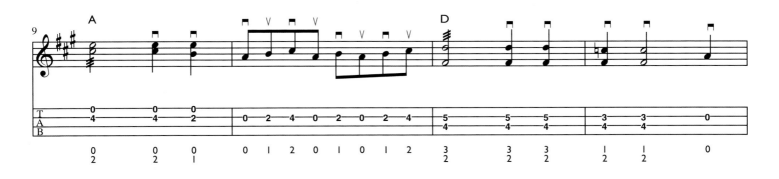

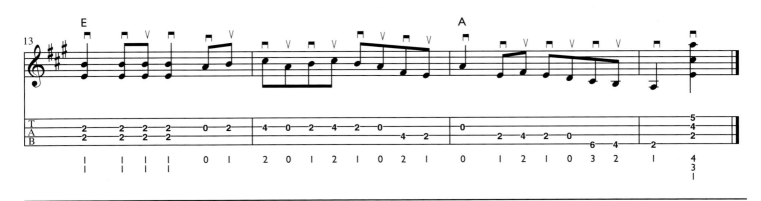

In an improvised break, you have total freedom to create new melodies and rhythmic ideas over the main chord progression. They can relate to the original melody, or go into whole new places. Insofar as improvised breaks are concerned, bluegrass is closely related to the blues and jazz traditions, where solos are an opportunity for the player to create something new on the spot that follows the chord progression the other musicians are playing.

TIPS FOR CREATING IMPROVISED BREAKS

- Use what you know. Every fiddle tune, folk song, bluegrass melody, or blues lick you have ever learned is available as inspiration for a break.

- Don't blow it all at once! Try using just a small number of ideas in your break. They can be repeated or altered through slight variations. This will help give your break a sense of tunefulness and structure, whereas just running unrelated scales and licks would likely not create a coherent solo. This will also help give each of your breaks for different songs their own identity and character.

- Experiment. Try new things all the time. If they don't work, find your way to something that will. This will lead you to sounds you never thought of that might be brilliant!

HOW TO MAKE THE MOST OUT OF A LITTLE

Here are some tips for "working" your ideas and licks to get the most out of them.

- **"Steal" the structure of the original melody.** One way to structure a break (or a phrase in a break) is to model it on the phrase lengths or rhythms of the original melody. In the following improvised break for "Free Little Bird" on page 49, the first two phrases (bars 1–8) mimic the original melody in that they start with the same basic notes, although they finish differently.

- **Reuse, recycle, renew!** While this is a sensible environmental policy, it's also a great musical policy. Try repeating a small two- or four-beat lick several times as the chords change in your break. You could repeat a lick two or three times and change how it ends the last time, or vary it as you go. Borrow licks from other tunes and sources. In the break on page 49, the third phrase (bars 9–12) borrows a melodic pattern you learned in the key of C Major for "Orville and Lloyd's Rag" (pages 36–37).

- **Patterns and sequences.** As mentioned above, the third phrase of the following example uses a rag-style lick on the A chord. It then repeats the lick one string lower on the D chord. The lick is used as a pattern that can be moved from chord to chord.

  Another way to use a pattern is as a *sequence*. In a sequence, a melodic idea is played, then its structure is duplicated starting on a different scale note (usually the adjacent note up or down). The sequencing can continue (up or down) for as long as you want. A great source for understanding sequences is the music of the Baroque master, Johann Sebastian Bach (1685–1750). An example of sequencing appears in bars 13–14 of the break on page 49.

Here is an improvised break for "Free Little Bird." On the CD that is included with this book, you will hear this break first, then you will hear just the chords so that you can practice your own breaks.

FREE LITTLE BIRD—IMPROVISED BREAK

Track 45

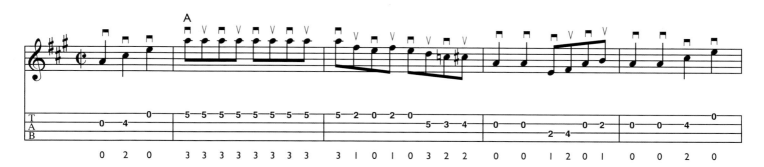

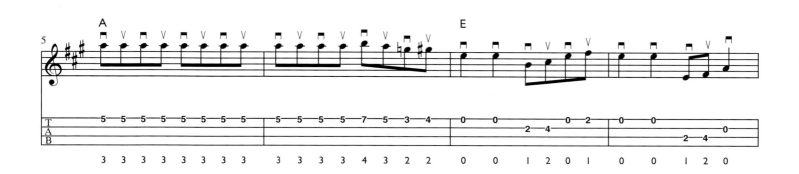

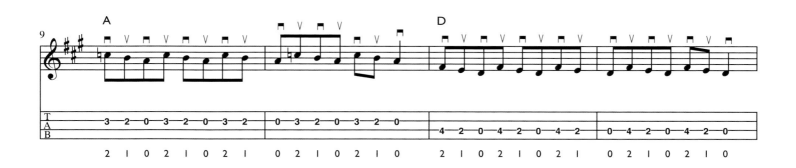

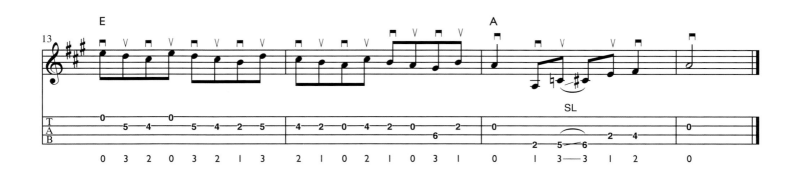

CHAPTER 6

Working Up the Neck

LESSON 1: MOVEABLE MAJOR SCALES

Whether you play bluegrass, jazz or rock, at some point you're going to want to play in something other than the easy open keys of G, D, A and C. The first step to playing in new keys is to learn how to play major scales that can be moved to any point on the neck (using no open strings).

As you learned in *Beginning Mandolin* (page 80), the major scale is the foundation of the language of music theory. It is the "default setting" or "home base" for the basic scale degrees of 1, 2, 3, 4, 5, 6 and 7. You will play many other scales and structures, but they will always be explained in terms that relate back to the original major scale structure of "whole step, whole step, half step, whole step, whole step, whole step, half step."

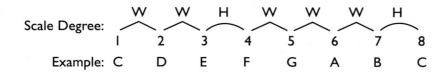

There are four basic fingerings for a one-octave major scale, one beginning on each of the left-hand fingers. This lesson will use the key of C Major to illustrate all four fingerings. While it is easy to play in C Major in an open position, this key is also useful for illustrating positions up the neck. The key of C Major has no sharps or flats, which makes it easy to keep track of the notes you are playing as you learn.

Moveable Major Scale, Start 1—Starting with the 1st Finger
Here is a C Major scale starting with the 1st finger at the 5th fret on the 4th string. This same pattern could also start an octave higher with the 1st finger at the 3rd fret of the 2nd string; the finger pattern would remain the same.

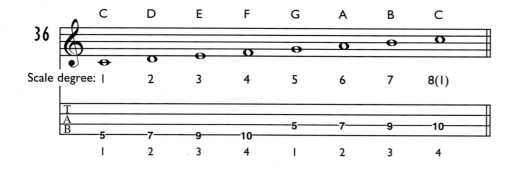

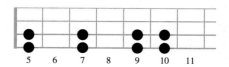

When you learn a new scale or fingering, it is important to spend time playing melodies and improvising within the fingering. This is how you will get to know it well. Here is an example to try using Start 1.

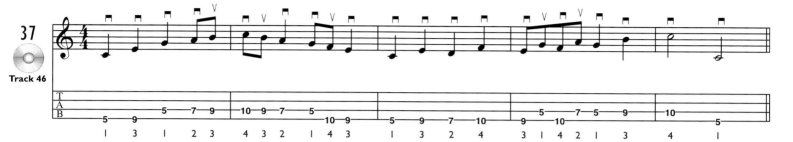

Moveable Major Scale, Start 2—Starting with the 2nd Finger

Here's the fingering for a C Major scale starting with the 2nd finger on the 5th fret of the 4th string. This pattern could also be played an octave higher starting with the 2nd finger on the 3rd fret of the 2nd string.

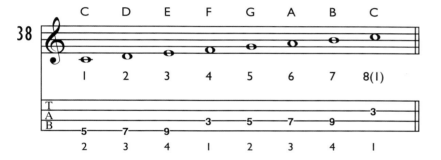
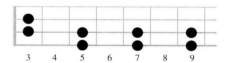

Here's an example to practice this fingering.

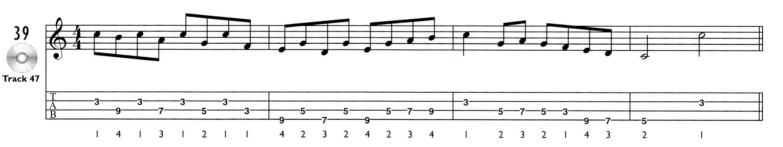

Here are the other two fingerings for a moveable major scale. Be sure to spend some time playing melodies and improvising licks in each fingering.

Moveable Major Scale, Start 3—Starting with the 3rd Finger

Here is the C Major scale starting with the 3rd finger on the 5th fret of the 4th string. This fingering could also start an octave higher with the 3rd finger on the 10th fret of the 3rd string.

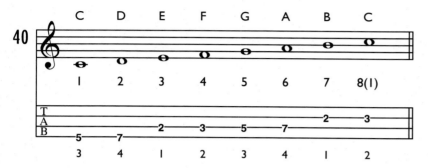
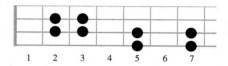

Moveable Major Scale, Start 4—Starting with the 4th Finger

Here is the C Major scale starting with the 4th finger on the 10th fret of the 3rd string.

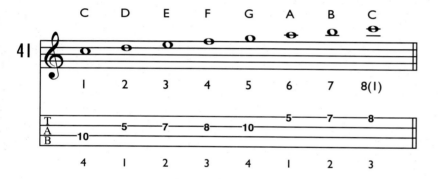
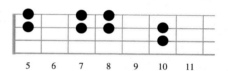

CONNECTING MAJOR SCALE FINGERINGS

Once you are familiar with the four one-octave fingerings, it is easy to string them together across the neck. There is even a formula you can use to remember the connections, just think "starting finger minus one." Here's how it works.

START 4 connects to START 3
START 3 connects to START 2
START 2 connects to START 1
START 1 connects to START 4

Start 4 Connecting to Start 3

Here is a C Major scale starting with the 4th finger on the 17th fret (way up there!) of the 4th string. The second octave begins with the 3rd finger on the 15th fret of the 2nd string. Do you recognize both patterns?

8va = Notes sound one octave higher than written

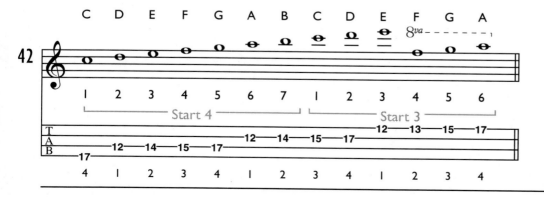
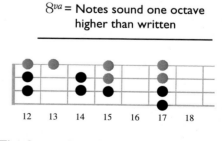

The finger-placement dots are shown in different colors to indicate where one fingering stops and another starts.

Start 3 Connecting to Start 2

This C Major scale starts with the 3rd finger on the 5th fret of the 4th string. The second octave begins with the 2nd finger on the 3rd fret of the 2nd string.

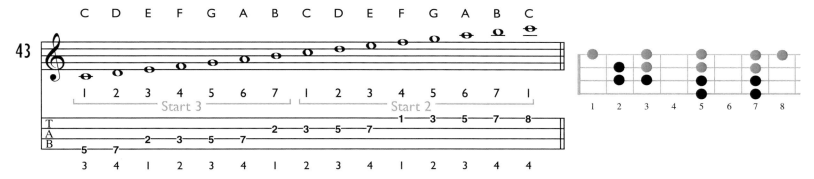

Start 2 Connecting to Start 1

Here is a C Major scale starting with the 2nd finger on the 5th fret of the 4th string. The second octave begins with the 1st finger on the 3rd fret of the 2nd string.

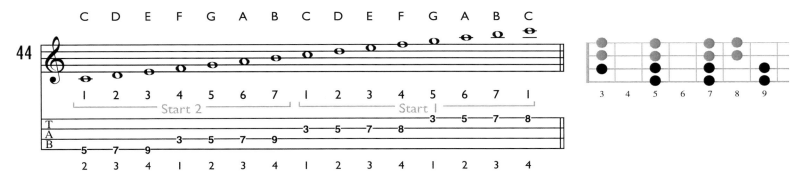

Start 1 Connecting to Start 4

This is a C Major scale starting with the 1st finger on the 5th fret of the 4th string. The second octave begins with the 4th finger on the 10th fret of the 3rd string.

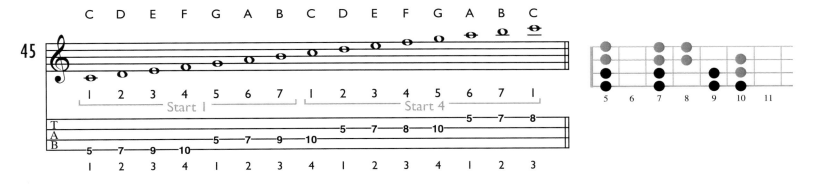

Another Approach: Start 1 Connecting to Start 3

Below is a fingering used very often in bluegrass and blues improvisation. When you reach the end of the first octave, slide your 3rd finger up from the 7th degree to the 1st degree of the next octave. This fingering connects two of the easiest, most agile one-octave fingerings.

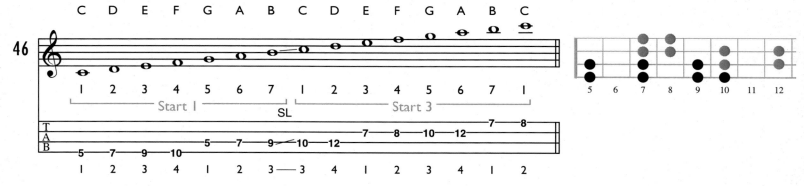

Here is an example of improvisation using Start 1 Connecting to Start 3. The chord progression is set to a bluegrass beat and is inspired by the bluegrass standard, "Nine-Pound Hammer." Chord fingerings may be found on page 9. On the CD that is included with this book, you will hear this example, then the chord progression is repeated so that you can practice improvising with this fingering and all of the other fingerings in this lesson. Watch the left-hand fingerings carefully!

THIS HAMMER'S STILL TOO HEAVY

Track 48

In order to prepare for the following lessons on double stops and arpeggios, it is important to review the chords that are produced using the notes of the major scale.

DIATONIC HARMONY IN MAJOR KEYS

In *Beginning Mandolin* (page 88), you learned about three kinds of triads and how they are used to harmonize the major scale. Triads are chords using three notes: a root, a 3rd (the third scale note above the root) and a 5th (the fifth scale note above the root). The three kinds of triads found in major keys are major, minor and diminished. Below is a C Major scale harmonized in triads. The triads that are formed using the notes of the scale create the *diatonic harmony* for the key. Diatonic means "of the key." Since it is difficult to play the triads as written, sample chord fingerings are shown above so that you can hear the basic sound of the chords.

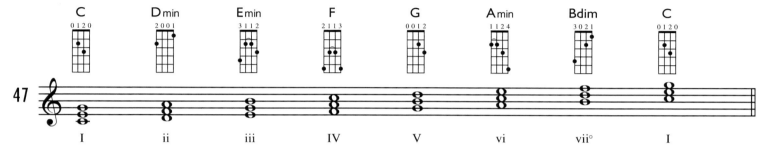

The triads are numbered with Roman numerals based on the scale degrees of the root notes. Upper-case Roman numerals designate major triads; lower-case numerals designate minor and diminished triads. Diminished triads are also marked with a small, open circle (○).

The major chords I, IV and V are considered the *primary chords* of the key. They impart the basic sound of the key, and are the most common chords in many blues, bluegrass and old-time tunes. You should memorize the primary chords of every key.

LEARNING THE CYCLE OF DIATONIC TRIADS IN ALL MAJOR KEYS

Let's call the diatonic triads for any major key played in numerical order *the cycle of diatonic triads*. The series can be memorized as: major–minor–minor–major–major–minor–diminished. Here are the diatonic triads in each major key.

Major Key	I	ii	iii	IV	V	vi	vii°
A	A	Bmin	C♯min	D	E	F♯min	G♯dim
B♭	B♭	Cmin	Dmin	E♭	F	Gmin	A dim
B	B	C♯min	D♯min	E	F♯	G♯min	A♯dim
C	C	Dmin	Emin	F	G	Amin	B dim
D♭	D♭	E♭min	Fmin	G♭	A♭	B♭min	C dim
D	D	Emin	F♯min	G	A	Bmin	C♯dim
E♭	E♭	Fmin	Gmin	A♭	B♭	Cmin	D dim
E	E	F♯min	G♯min	A	B	C♯min	D♯dim
F	F	Gmin	Amin	B♭	C	Dmin	E dim
G♭	G♭	A♭min	B♭min	C♭	D♭	E♭min	F dim
G	G	Amin	Bmin	C	D	Emin	F♯dim
A♭	A♭	B♭min	Cmin	D♭	E♭	Fmin	G dim

A double stop is two notes played simultaneously. The term comes from the violin family, where the maximum number of strings that can be played at once by the bow is two adjacent strings. The left hand fingers "stop" or finger the notes, hence the name "double stop."

Double stops are used on the mandolin to harmonize a melody. One way to harmonize a melody is in 3rds. To do this, you will need to be able to play major 3rds (M3) and minor 3rds (m3). For more on these and all of the other interval shapes, see pages 82–87 of *Beginning Mandolin*. Here are the fingerings for major and minor 3rds on each adjacent pair of mandolin strings.

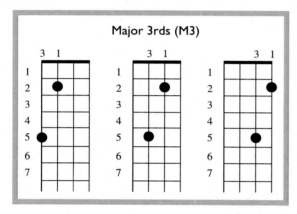

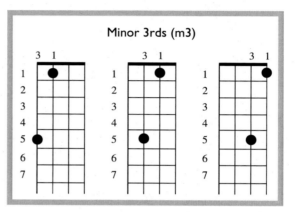

The most common way to harmonize a melody is to use the roots and 3rds of the cycle of diatonic triads. The melody note is the lower, or root note, and the harmony note is a 3rd above. You will know whether to use a major or minor 3rd by referring to the diatonic cycle: major–minor–minor–major–major–minor–diminished. The diminished chord uses a minor 3rd. Here is a D Major scale harmonized in 3rds on the first two strings.

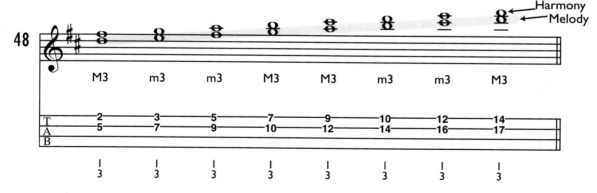

Try creating melodies that go up and down this cycle of 3rd intervals. Also try the same cycle of fingerings starting elsewhere on the neck (in other keys).

Here is a short exercise using double stops of major and minor 3rds. This should help you get used to the way the shapes cycle up and down the scale. This tune uses 3rds to evoke the music of Mexico and the American Southwest.

SAN ANTONIO SUNRISE

Track 49

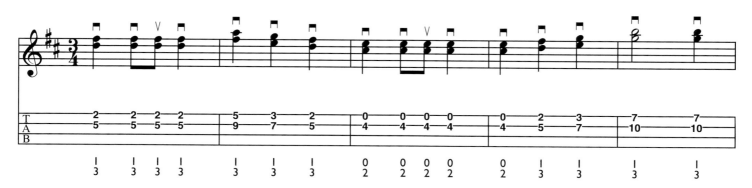

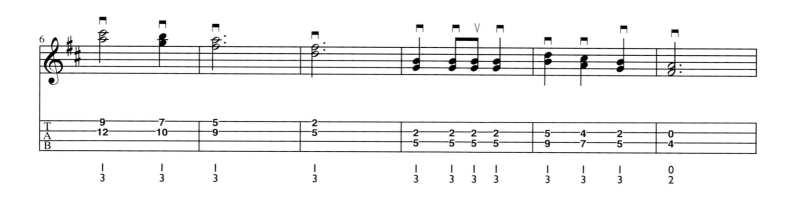

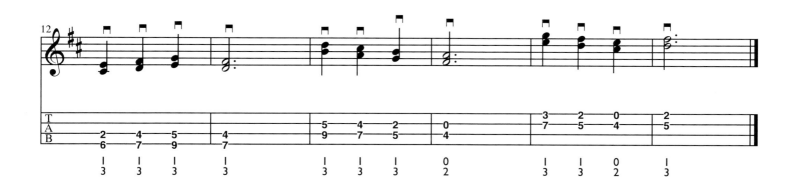

A WORLD TURNED UPSIDE-DOWN

A 6th is the *inversion* of a 3rd (for more on intervals and inversions, see page 82–87 of *Beginning Mandolin*). In other words, a 6th is a 3rd turned upside-down. For example, G to B is a major 3rd, while B to G is a minor 6th. When an interval is inverted, its quality (major or minor) is changed. So, keep in mind that *major* 3rds invert to *minor* 6ths, and *minor* 3rds invert to *major* 6ths. Here are fingerings for major 6ths (M6) and minor 6ths (m6).

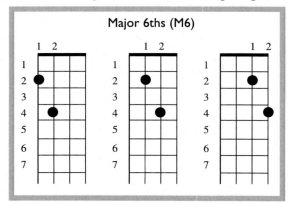
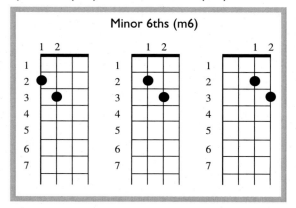

Below is a G Major scale harmonized in 6ths. The cycle still relates to the diatonic cycle. Now the roots are in the top voice, and the harmony is in the lower voice.

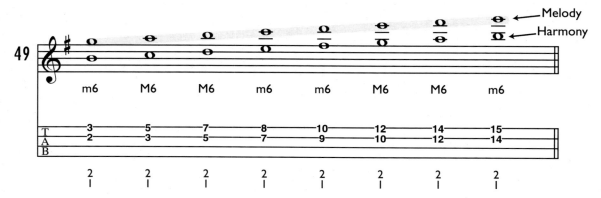

Harmonized 6ths have a more open, spread out sound than 3rds. Here is a move using 6ths that you can apply to any major chord. This is a very common sound on the mandolin. It is reminiscent of the guitar lick used in the intro to Van Morrison's "Brown Eyed Girl." Here it is shown for a G, C and D chord (I, IV and V in the key of G).

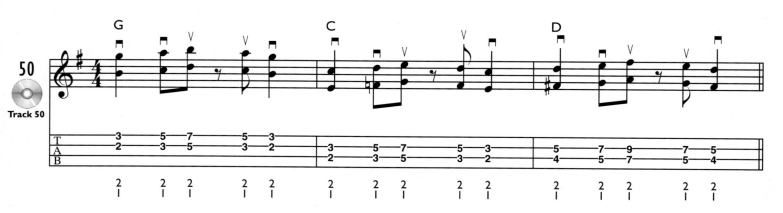

This tune uses 6ths played both simultaneously and broken up to evoke Hawaiian music and slide guitar. You will also slide 6ths from one position to another. This sound is also common in country, bluegrass and gospel. Notice the cool G6 chord at the end.

FINGERING ALERT: Sometimes you must adjust your fingerings to make the music flow better, or execute a move more comfortably. This exercise uses several ways of fingering the 6th shapes you have learned. Try them as written, or adapt your own fingerings to the TAB.

MANDOHULA SUNSET

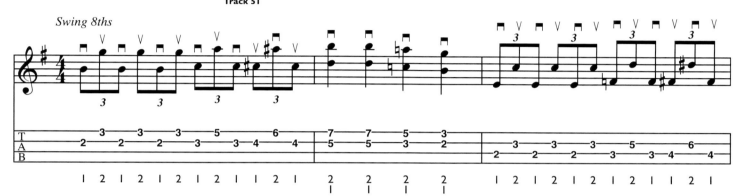

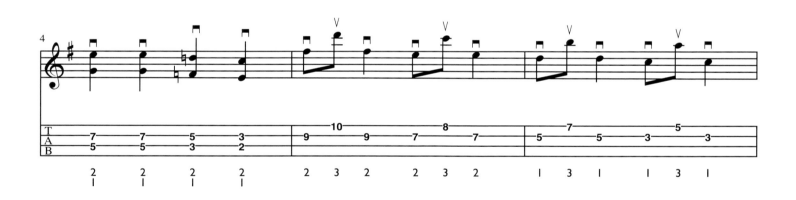

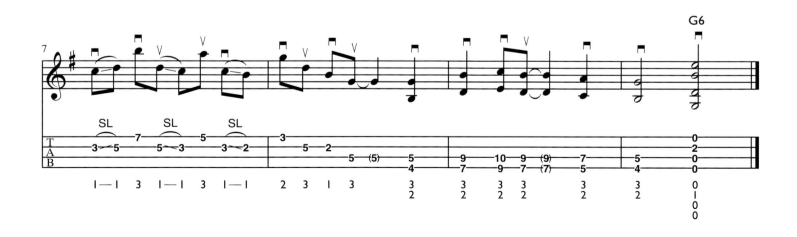

In *Beginning Mandolin* (page 76) you learned how to play open chords one string at a time to create arpeggio accompaniment patterns. In this lesson, you will learn how arpeggiated triads can spice up your improvisation and help you work up the neck.

The following arpeggio fingerings are shown for chords built on the root note C. This will help you see which notes are changing to form the different triads. Practice the fingerings going up and down, then try them on different root notes elsewhere on the neck. As you will see, these arpeggios are not the type played with each note on a different string.

MAJOR ARPEGGIO FINGERINGS

These fingerings for C Major arpeggios correspond directly to the scale fingerings you learned starting on page 50. The chord tones of root (R), 3rd (3) and 5th (5) are indicated.

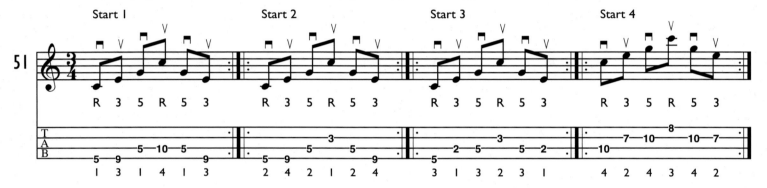

MINOR ARPEGGIO FINGERINGS

To make a C Minor triad arpeggio, simply lower the 3rds from the C Major arpeggios one half step to form minor 3rd chord tones (also called ♭3).

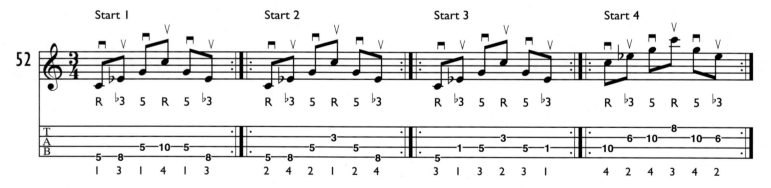

DIMINISHED ARPEGGIO FINGERINGS

Now try a C Diminished triad arpeggio. You must lower both the 3rd and 5th of a major triad to form the minor 3rd (♭3) and diminished 5th (♭5) chord tones.

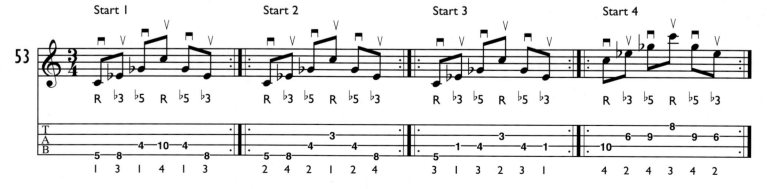

DIATONIC ARPEGGIOS IN C MAJOR

You can use the arpeggio fingerings you have learned to outline all of the triads in any major key. Here is one way to do the diatonic triads in the key of C. You will find many more possible fingerings if you try the chords on different strings starting with different fingers.

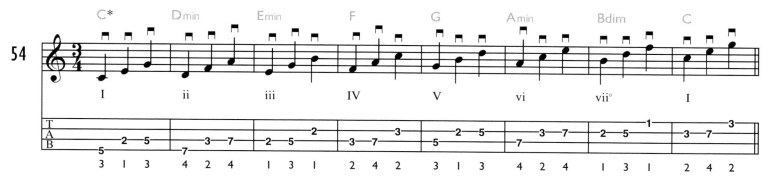

Arpeggios are used heavily in improvisation and within the melodies of tunes. Jazz and swing tunes often use arpeggios. Irish jigs are among the fiddle tunes that use arpeggios (see "Money in Both Pockets" and "Scatter the Mud" on pages 40 and 41). Even one of your first fiddle tunes, "Soldier's Joy" (*Beginning Mandolin* page 37) is built on a D Major arpeggio. Here's a tune that will give you a chance to practice arpeggio fingerings.

SATURDAY NIGHT AT THE GULAG ARPEGGIO

Track 52

---

* The chord symbols are gray because while they are here to indicate which chord is being arpeggiated, they do not imply that an accompaniment is needed or present.

LESSON 6: ARPEGGIOS—AUGMENTED TRIADS AND SEVENTH CHORDS

There is one more triad type yet to learn: the *augmented* triad. Augmented triads do not occur in the diatonic cycle of a major key, but they are sometimes used to add a new flavor to a chord progression. An augmented triad is constructed with two major 3rds stacked on top of the root. In other words, an augmented triad is a major triad with a raised 5th (♯5). Here are the fingerings for augmented arpeggios built on C.

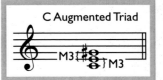

AUGMENTED ARPEGGIO FINGERINGS

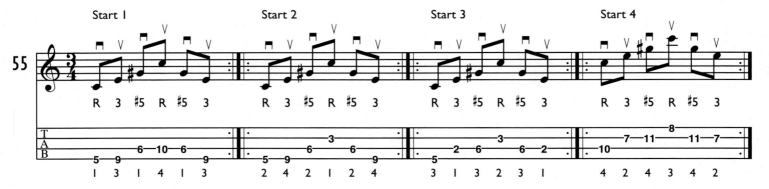

7TH CHORDS

When you add one more 3rd to your triad stack (root–3rd–5th), you get a seventh chord (root–3rd–5th–7th). There are five types of 7th chords. Here they are shown built on the root note C.

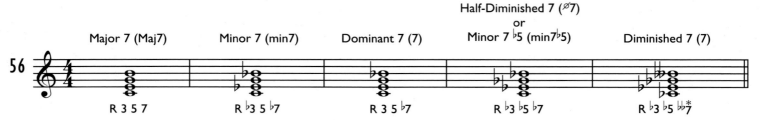

7th chord arpeggios are very important in blues, jazz and Brazilian mandolin music. This lesson will cover the three most common 7th chords: the major 7 (Maj7), minor 7 (min7) and dominant-7 (7) arpeggios. You can use your knowledge of the other chord structures shown above to adapt these fingerings for half-diminished and diminished 7 chords.

MAJOR 7 ARPEGGIO FINGERINGS

Major 7 chords use the root (R), 3rd (3), 5th (5) and 7th (7) from the major scale. Here are fingerings for a CMaj7 arpeggio. Major 7 chords occur on the I and IV chords of a major key.

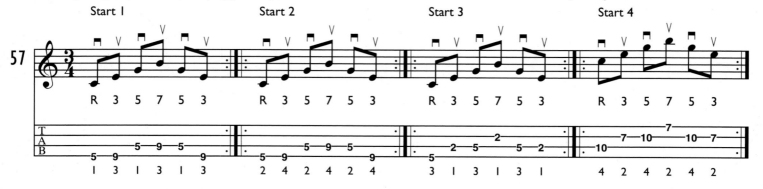

---

* ♭♭ = *Double flat.* Lowers the note a whole step.

MINOR 7 ARPEGGIO FINGERINGS

Minor 7 chords (min7) are made with a minor triad plus a minor 7th interval. The structure is root (R), minor 3rd (♭3), 5th (5) and minor 7th (♭7). Minor 7 chords occur on the ii, iii and vi chords of a major key (for example, Dmin7, Emin7 and Amin7 in the key of C). Below are fingerings for a Cmin7 arpeggio. Learn and compare them with the major 7 and dominant-7 fingerings.

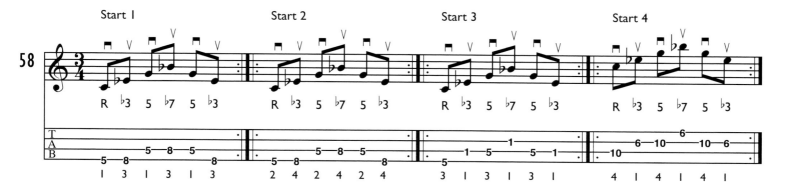

DOMINANT 7 ARPEGGIO FINGERINGS

The dominant 7 chord (indicated in music by the root and the 7, as in "C7") is a major triad plus a minor 7 interval. A dominant-7 chord is so named because it occurs on the V chord of a major key, which is also called the *dominant* chord. Here are the fingerings for C7 arpeggios. C7 is the V chord in the key of F, which has a key signature with one flat (B♭).

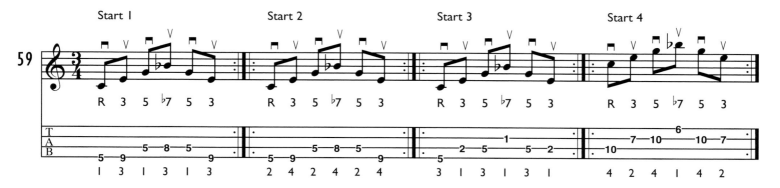

Here is a short chord progression using arpeggios for CMaj7, Amin7 and G7.

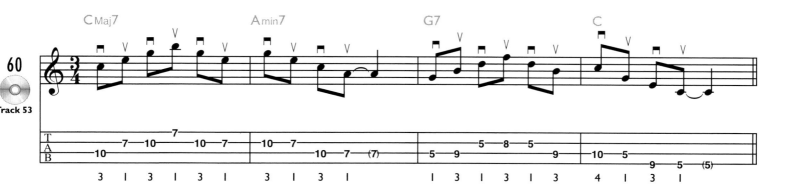

On page 70 of *Beginning Mandolin*, you learned that a natural minor scale is made by lowering the 3rd ($\flat$3), 6th ($\flat$6) and 7th ($\flat$7) of a major scale. There are many other possible types of minor scales. The natural minor scale, one of the most common minor scales, has two other names: the *relative minor* scale and the *Aeolian mode*. All three of these names denote the same scale.

The natural minor scale can be formed by starting on the 6th scale degree of a major scale. For example, in a C Major scale, the 6 is A. By starting a new scale on A, using the same notes, you create an A Natural Minor scale.

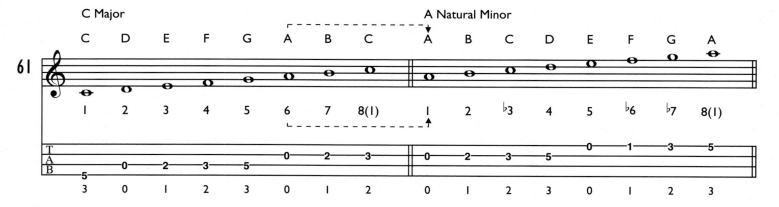

HANGING WITH THE RELATIVES
AROUND THE BIG CIRCLE

Since the A Natural Minor scale and the C Major scale have the same notes, they are said to be *relative minor* and *relative major* to one another. All major keys have a relative minor starting on the 6th note of the scale. Likewise, all minor keys have a relative major starting on the 3rd note. Here is the circle of 5ths (see *Beginning Mandolin*, page 81) shown with major and relative minor keys and the key signatures they share.

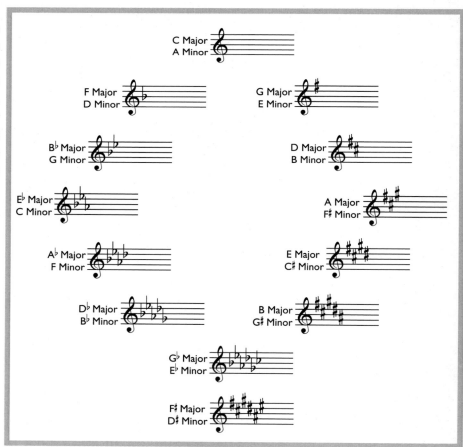

Now let's look again at the A Natural Minor scale. It helps to compare it to the A Major scale. We see that the A Major scale has a C♯, an F♯ and a G♯. The A Natural Minor scale, since it shares notes with C Major, has C♮ F♮ and G♮. In other words, the natural minor scale has a lowered 3rd (♭3), a lowered 6th (♭6) and a lowered 7th (♭7) when compared to a major scale built on the same note (called the *tonic*). Here is one octave for each scale for you to compare.

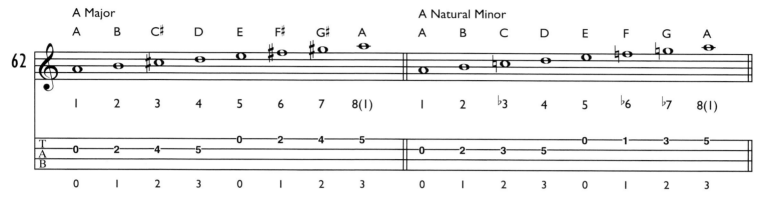

DIATONIC HARMONY OF THE NATURAL MINOR SCALE

Here is an A Natural Minor scale shown with triads built on each note. Sample mandolin fingerings are shown above the chords. The fingerings do not produce the chord tones exactly as written, but will help you hear the sound of the chord cycle. This cycle (minor–diminished–major–minor–minor–major–minor) is found in every natural minor key.

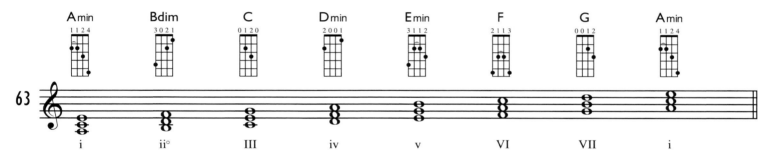

You can form moveable minor scales by lowering the 3rd, 6th and 7th of your major scale fingerings from page 50–54. Here is a short tune using the A Natural Minor scale in open position (shown in example 62, above). Chords are indicated, use a simple bluegrass strum for rhythm (page 42) with the fingerings shown in example 63, above.

TOULOUSE LAUTREC

Track 54

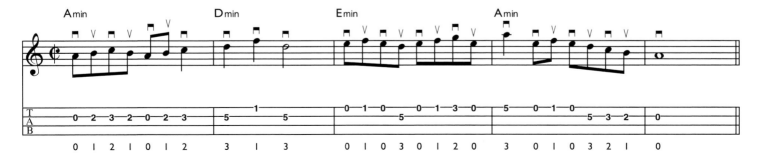

CHAPTER 7

Blues and Bluegrass Improv Up the Neck

This chapter will use the blues and bluegrass to help you work on your improvisation skills up the neck. You will learn how to use the minor pentatonic and major pentatonic scales in the key of B Major, with fingerings that can be moved to any other key on the neck. Work through this chapter even if you are interested in styles other than blues or bluegrass, as the scales, chords and skills involved are fundamental to all styles of music.

LESSON 1: MOVEABLE DOMINANT 7 CHORDS

On page 62–63, you learned arpeggio fingerings for dominant 7 chords. A dominant 7 chord includes a root (R), major 3rd (3), perfect 5th (5) and minor 7th (♭7). Below are some good moveable mandolin fingerings for dominant 7 chords. They can be moved all over the neck to form any dominant 7 chord. Simply move the fingering up or down to any root you desire. For example, a B7 chord could be moved up one half-step (one fret) to form a C7 chord or down one fret to form a B♭7.

The top row of fingerings are very common and easy to play. The fingerings in the bottom row are a bit more challenging, but can come in handy in some tight situations.

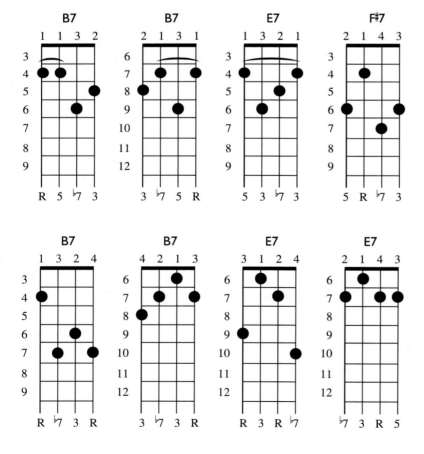

Below is a blues shuffle strum in swing 8ths. Try it with any of the fingerings shown on page 66.

Blues Shuffle Strum

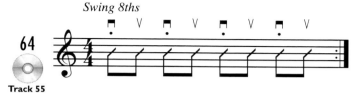

Track 55

Now try this 12-bar blues (*Beginning Mandolin*, page 52) using dominant 7 chords in the key of B. On pages 62–63 of this book, you learned that the dominant 7 chord only occurs on the V chord of a major key. The blues, however, plays by different rules. Because of the addition of extra "blue" notes to the major scale, the dominant 7 chord can be used on the I, IV and V chord as you like.

Suggested chord voicings are shown. You can use the blues shuffle strum above, or try it with a bluegrass rhythm. The I, IV and V chords are marked below the staff to help you memorize the 12-bar blues form.

BLUES IN MY BEE BONNET (OR, BEES IN MY BLUE BONNET)

Track 56

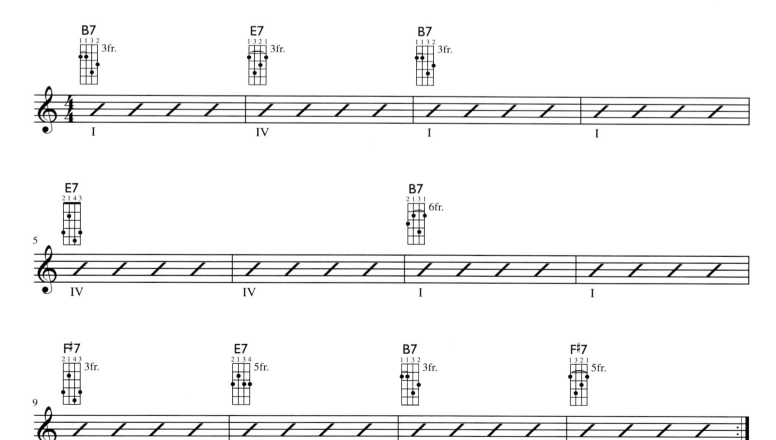

The minor pentatonic scale was introduced in *Beginning Mandolin* as a good scale for modal fiddle tunes (page 44) and for blues improvisation (page 56). Pentatonic means "five notes." The minor pentatonic scale has five scale degrees: 1, ♭3, 4, 5 and ♭7 (as always, the numbers correspond to notes in the major scale). This scale does not have scale degrees 2 or 6. Here is a comparison of the notes and intervals found in the B Major and B Minor Pentatonic scales.

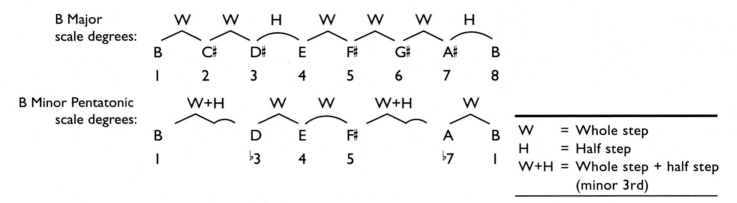

THE MINOR PENTATONIC INTERVAL SERIES

The minor pentatonic interval series is made up of whole steps and minor 3rds (whole step plus half step, W+H). The series found in the minor pentatonic scale (W+H–W–W–W+H–W) is very common in folk music from many cultures. Some of the earliest melodies known are in pentatonic scales.

USING PENTATONIC FINGERINGS AS "LANDMARKS"

By mastering the pentatonic fingerings shown in this lesson and the one on Major Pentatonic Scales (page 74), you can develop a "skeleton" or "outline" approach to learning the fretboard. The notes in the pentatonic scales become like landmarks, or basic tones common to many scales. This makes it easier to fill in the gaps with other scale tones you will learn about in the future.

WHEN TO USE THE MINOR PENTATONIC SCALE

Minor Keys: The minor pentatonic shares notes in common with many minor scales, particularly the natural minor (see page 64) and the Dorian mode (page 28). So the minor pentatonic will fit well in most minor keys (songs where the tonic chord (i) is minor).

Major Keys with Blue Notes: The ♭3 and ♭7 notes of the minor pentatonic could also be considered blue notes, or notes from a minor scale played against chords in a major key. This adds an emotional mood to the melody, which is part of the blues sound. This is also what puts the "blue" in "bluegrass." Whether or not this is the sound you want for a particular musical moment is a matter of taste and experimentation.

The fingerings in this lesson are shown starting on B, but can be moved to other keys by simply playing the pattern starting on other notes. Be sure to practice improvising and constructing melodies with each fingering. You could also use "Blues in my Bee Bonnet" (page 67) as a backup progression to practice improvising over.

Moveable Minor Pentatonic, Start 1—Starting with the 1st Finger

Below is a B Minor Pentatonic scale starting with the 1st finger on the 4th string. The pattern can be used in higher octaves by starting with the 1st finger on the 9th fret of the 3rd string or with the 1st finger on the 2nd fret of the 2nd string.

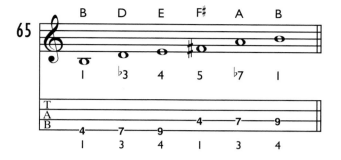
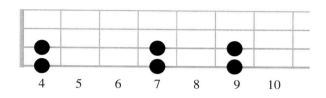

Improv Tip: Keep Track of the Tonic Note (Scale Degree 1)

A good way to start building licks in new scales is to construct licks that come to rest on the 1st scale degree. This helps you hear how the other notes in the scale are relating to the key. Using this concept, build small musical thoughts that end on 1 and then wait a bit before beginning the next thought. Here are a couple of examples.

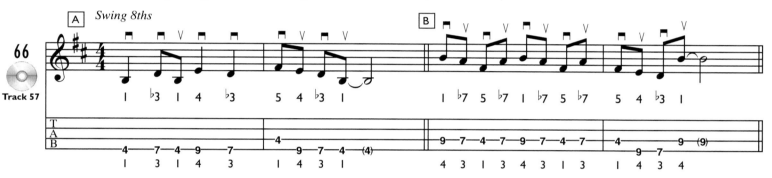

Moveable Minor Pentatonic, Start 2—Starting with the 2nd Finger

Below is a B Minor Pentatonic fingering starting with the 2nd finger on the 4th fret of the 4th string. The pattern can be used in higher octaves by starting with the 2nd finger on the 9th fret of the 3rd string or the 2nd finger on the 2nd fret of the 2nd string.

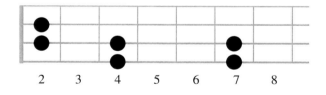

Here's a bluegrass style example. Chords are shown so that you can see how the licks fit over the chords. To play the chords, use the fingerings you learned on page 66.

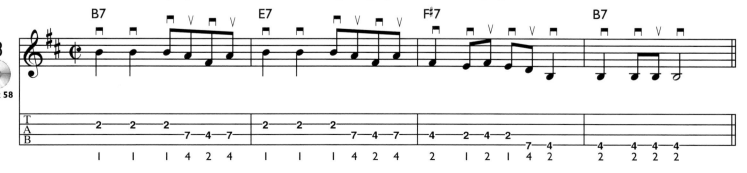

Moveable Minor Pentatonic, Start 3/4—Starting with the 3rd or 4th Finger

Here is a B Minor Pentatonic fingering starting with the 3rd finger on the 9th fret of the 3rd string.

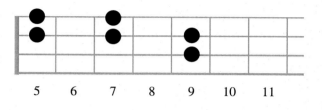

> **FINGERING ALERT: Two Fingerings for the Price of One!** The Start 3 fingering of the minor pentatonic scale can also be fingered starting with the 4th finger. Following is the B Minor Pentatonic Start 4 fingering.

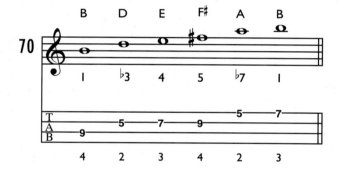

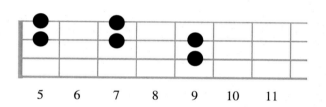

This example is set over chords in the key of B Minor (the relative minor of D Major, hence two sharps in the key signature). Chord fingerings are shown. Notice how the character of the scale changes depending on the quality (major or minor) of the backup chords. This example uses the Start 3 fingering, but you can also try it with Start 4.

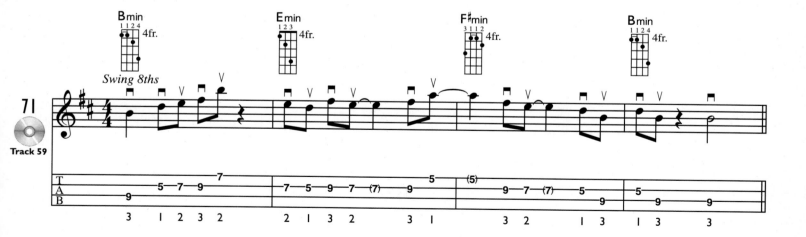

To create two-octave scale fingerings that go across the strings, you can connect the one-octave fingerings you have learned.

START 1 CONNECTING TO START 3/4

The most common way to extend the Start 1 fingering is to use a position *shift* (change) with the 3rd finger. This is shown in the TAB as a slide, but does not have to be articulated that way (it doesn't have to *sound* like a slide). Another way to finger the scale is to start the second octave with the 4th finger. Both possibilities are shown below.

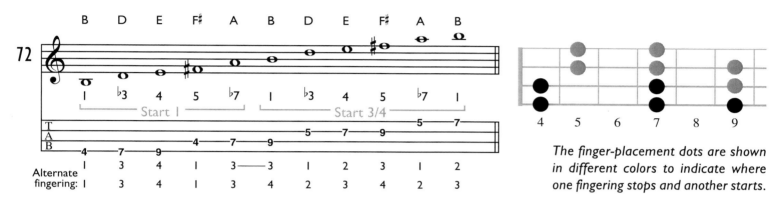

The finger-placement dots are shown in different colors to indicate where one fingering stops and another starts.

This example allows you to practice improvising over a simple bluegrass progression using the I, IV and V chords in B (B, E and F#). On the CD that is included with this book, you will hear the example as shown, then the chord progression will repeat so that you can practice your own improvisation.

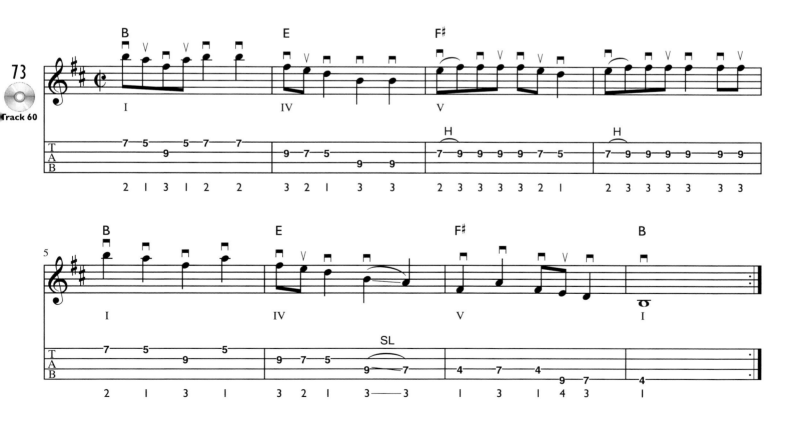

START 2 CONNECTING TO START 1

Here, the B Minor Pentatonic starts with the 2nd finger on the 4th fret of the 4th string and connects with the fingering that starts with the 1st finger on the 2nd fret of the 2nd string.

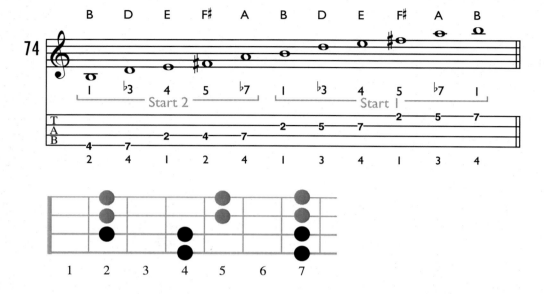

START 3 CONNECTING TO START 2

This fingering is not terribly convenient in the key of B, since it has to be placed so high on the neck. Once you learn the shapes of all these fingerings, try them in different keys. Some fingerings suit certain keys better than others. This one starts with the 3rd finger on the 16th fret of the 4th string and connects to the fingering that starts with the 2nd finger on the 14th fret of the 2nd string.

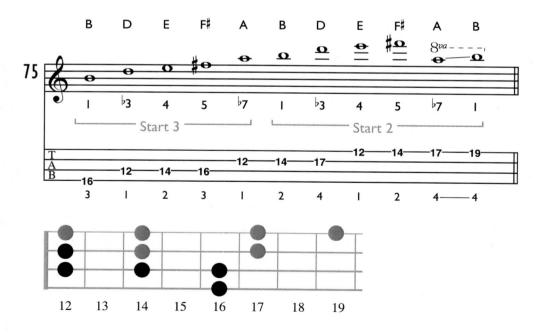

As stated earlier, you could use "Blues in My Bee Bonnet" (page 67) as a backup progression to practice your new scale fingerings. Here is a 12-bar blues in B Minor, using the minor i (Bmin), iv (Emin) and v (F#min) chords with a sample solo using some of the scale fingerings you have learned. On the CD that is available for this book, this tune is set in a medium bluegrass tempo and the chord progression is repeated for you to practice improvising over. Also try it using other grooves and tempos you like.

YOU WON'T B-MINOR FOREVER

Track 61

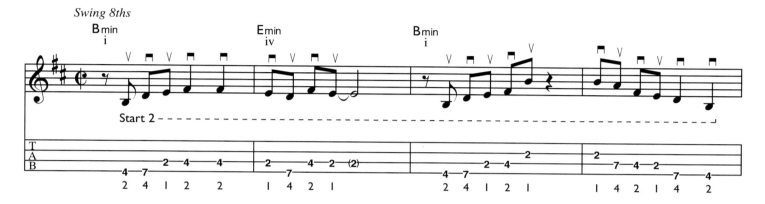

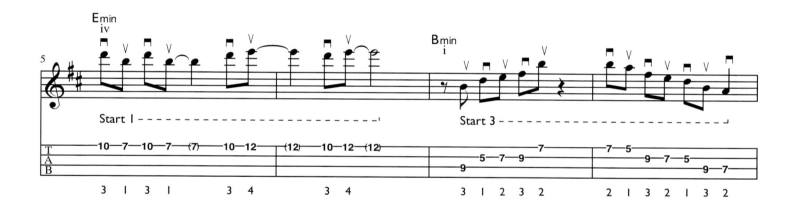

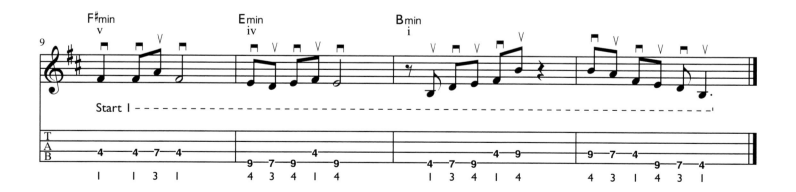

LESSON 4: THE MAJOR PENTATONIC SCALE

The *major pentatonic* scale is the friendlier, more optimistic sibling to the minor pentatonic scale. A huge number of vocal melodies used in folk songs and bluegrass songs are in the major pentatonic scale. The major pentatonic scale can be thought of as an "abbreviated" major scale. It contains scale degrees 1, 2, 3, 5 and 6, leaving out scale degrees 4 and 7. Here is a comparison of the interval structure and notes of the B Major scale and the B Major Pentatonic scale.

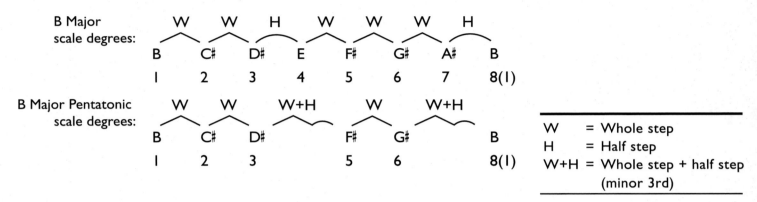

W	= Whole step					
H	= Half step					
W+H	= Whole step + half step (minor 3rd)					

NOT JUST SIBLINGS, TWINS!

Look closely at the interval structure of the major pentatonic scale (W–W–W+H–W–W+H). If you rotate this series four places (in other words, start the series on the last W+H interval and repeat the series from there) you get the series that makes up the minor pentatonic (W+H–W–W–W+H–W). The major and minor pentatonic are just two expressions of the same basic pentatonic interval series. This will make the major pentatonic fingerings seem familiar, especially as you connect them together.

There's another way to look at this relationship. Below are the notes of the A Minor Pentatonic scale and the C Major Pentatonic scale. They have exactly the same notes! It's just like the relationship between the A Natural Minor scale and the C Major scale. The A Minor Pentatonic scale is the *relative minor pentatonic* scale to the C Major Pentatonic Scale.

A Minor Pentatonic	A	C	D	E	G	
C Major Pentatonic		C	D	E	G	A

WHEN TO USE THE MAJOR PENTATONIC SCALE

Major Keys: The major pentatonic scale suits songs where the tonic chord (I) is major. As you learn more scales, you will learn scales other than the major scale that also use a major I chord. The major pentatonic scale suits most of these scales as well. The major pentatonic scale has an open, tuneful sound heard in country and bluegrass licks. This grouping of notes makes a particularly good scale for improvisation because it avoids the 4th and 7th degrees, which occasionally clash with certain chords in the key.

Moveable Major Pentatonic, Start 1—Starting with the 1st Finger

You will recognize this fingering from its similarity to the Start 1 fingering of the major scale (page 50). Here it is in the key of B Major.

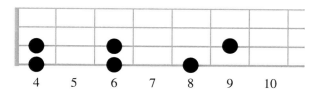

Here is a fiddle tune-style lick using the B Major Pentatonic Start 1 fingering.

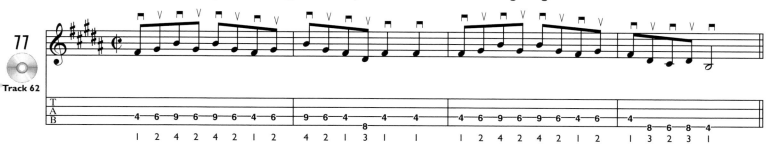

Moveable Major Pentatonic, Start 2—Starting with the 2nd Finger

Below is the B Major Pentatonic scale starting with the 2nd finger on the 4th fret of the 4th string. Note that this is just a slight variation of the Start 1 fingering, placing the final B-note (the start of the next octave) on the 2nd string instead of the 3rd string.

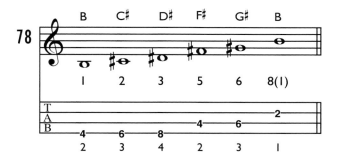

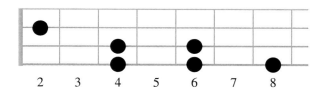

Try this example using Start 2.

Moveable Major Pentatonic Start 3—Starting with the 3rd Finger

This fingering is shown starting with the 3rd finger on the 9th fret of the 3rd string.

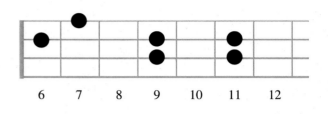

Notice how easily you can locate a major arpeggio (see page 60) within this fingering. Simply pick out the 1st, 3rd and 5th scale degrees. This example incorporates the B Major arpeggio using the B Major Pentatonic Start 3 fingering.

Moveable Major Pentatonic, Start 4—Starting with the 4th Finger

Here is a B Major Pentatonic scale starting with the 4th finger on the 9th fret of the 3rd string.

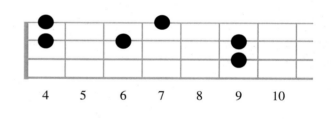

Try this example.

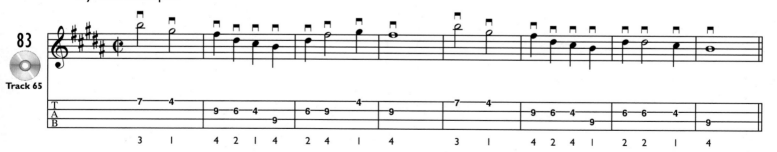

CONNECTING THE POSITIONS

The one-octave major pentatonic fingerings connect the same way the major scales did (page 52). Here are the two-octave moveable major pentatonic fingerings for the key of B Major. Practice them as scales going up and down, then use them to improvise and construct melodies.

Start 4 Connecting to Start 3

The finger-placement dots are shown in different colors to indicate where one fingering stops and another starts.

Start 3 Connecting to Start 2

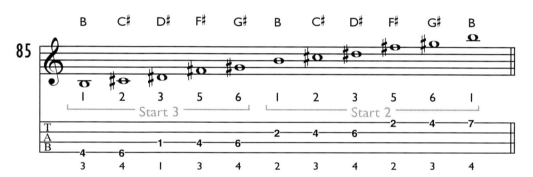
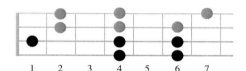

Start 2 Connecting to Start 1

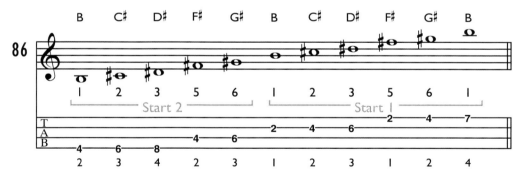
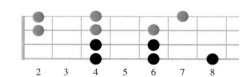

Start 1 Connecting to Start 4

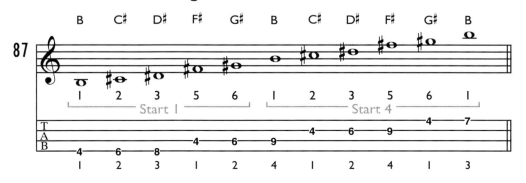
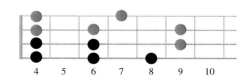

The sample solos in this lesson are based on an *8-bar blues* chord progression. There are several formulas used for the 8-bar blues. This particular progression can be heard in the blues standard "Key to the Highway" by Big Bill Broonzy. The chords are indicated and chord analysis shown so that you can play this progression in other keys. On the CD included with this book, each solo will be followed by a repeat of the chord progression so that you can practice your own soloing.

This solo uses the B Major Pentatonic in the "Start 1 Connecting to Start 4" fingering (page 77).

KEY TO THE HIGH SCHOOL—SOLO NO. 1 (MAJOR PENTATONIC)
Track 66

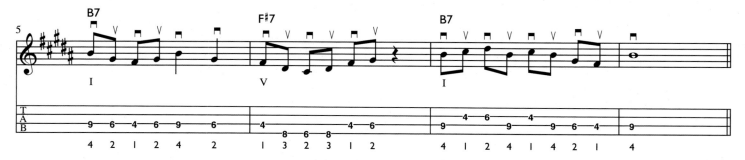

Try this solo over the same chord progression using the B Minor Pentatonic scale ("Start 1 Connecting to Start 3" fingering, page 71). Listen to how the blue notes in the scale change the emotional character of the solo.

KEY TO THE HIGH SCHOOL—SOLO NO. 2 (MINOR PENTATONIC)
Track 67

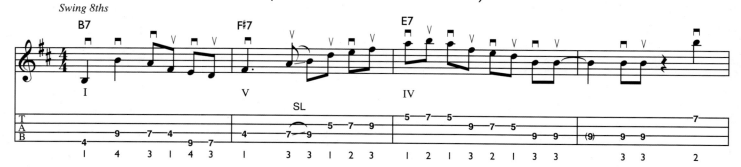

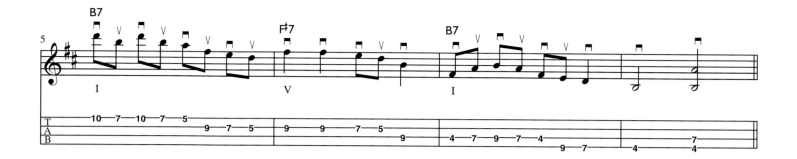

The next solo mixes the minor and major pentatonic scales in the same solo. Notice how the major pentatonic scale sounds great over the initial I and V chords, while the minor pentatonic helps lead the ear to the IV chord. This is because the ♭3 of the minor pentatonic scale (a D note in the key of B) is the same note as the ♭7 chord tone of the IV chord (a D note in the E7 chord). Also, the minor pentatonic scale includes the 4th scale degree, the root of the IV chord. While there is no rule that says the major pentatonic scale goes over the I and V, and the minor goes over the IV, it is interesting that the scales can suggest these changes because of the chord tones within the scale.

KEY TO THE HIGH SCHOOL—SOLO NO. 3 (MAJOR AND MINOR PENTATONIC)

Track 68

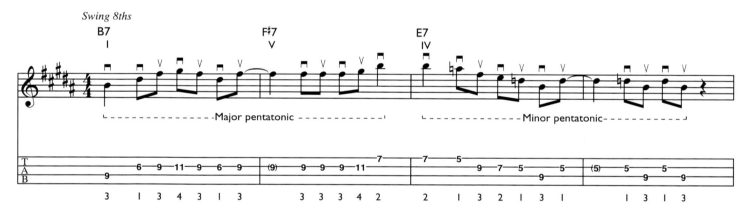

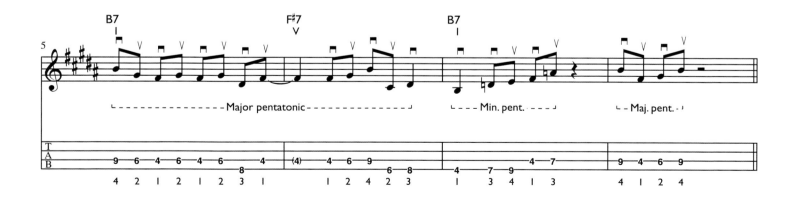

CHAPTER 8

A Taste of Swing and Jazz Mandolin

The mandolin has always had a foothold in the world of swing and jazz music. The black string bands of the early 20th century often had mandolinists playing their vast repertoires of dixieland, swing and other jazz and blues tunes. Later players such as Dave Apollon used the mandolin as a vehicle for virtuosic improvisation. No single player has done more to bring together swing and the mandolin than David "Dawg" Grisman. His patented "Dawg Music" sound incorporates influences from swing, bluegrass, Brazilian music and anything else to which Grisman takes a liking.

LESSON 1: SWING RHYTHM PLAYING

BASIC SWING STRUM

The most traditional swing rhythm pattern is to strum percussive, clipped (staccato) chords in a quarter-note rhythm. Guitarist Freddie Green was a master of this style. Try the following progression. The downstrokes are just like the bluegrass "chop" strum. Use your left hand to cut the chords short by slightly releasing the pressure on the strings. This strum also incorporates a soft upstroke at the end of the bar.

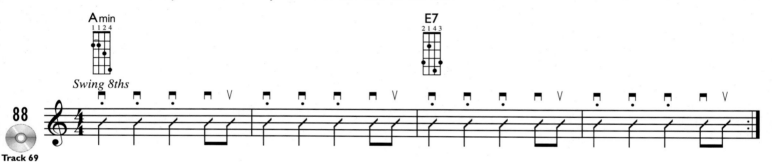

HOT GYPSY RHYTHM STRUM

This approach to swing rhythm draws inspiration from the "hot jazz" of gypsy guitarist Django Reinhardt.

THE 32-BAR SONG FORM

The *32-bar song form* is found in countless jazz tunes (known as *standards*). It is an old pop song form in which a melody lasting eight bars (the "A" section of the song) is played twice, then a contrasting "B" section of eight bars is played and finally followed by a repeat of the A section. This A–A–B–A form is repeated as many times as the musicians want, and is used for both the melody (called the *head*) and the improvised solos. In jazz lingo, each repetition is called a *chorus*.

Here is a chord progression using the strum patterns you have learned (watch out for a couple of variations!). It is a simple 32-bar song form. The return of the A section is indicated by *D.C. al Fine*, which means to repeat from the top until the finish (*Fine*).

SWING BY YOUR THUMBS (SIMPLE RHYTHM CHORDS)

Now that you've got the basic sound of "Swing By Your Thumbs" in your ears, it's time to spice things up with some more colorful chords. Jazz players add 7ths, 6ths and even more extended chord tones to basic triads to make the harmony more rich and complex. Some of the great swing players change chord voicings on nearly every beat!

MAJOR 7 CHORDS

As you learned on page 62, a major 7 chord (Maj7) is constructed using the root (R), 3rd (3), 5th (5) and 7th (7) of a major scale. You can find voicings for major 7 chords on your mandolin by using your regular major triad fingerings. Find a root in the fingering, and lower it by one half step. This note is the major 7th chord tone. Here are some moveable fingerings with the chord tones shown under the diagrams. Some of these fingerings are very tricky. Learn the ones that work best for you.

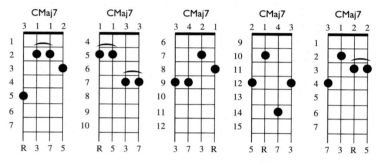

MINOR 7 CHORDS

The minor 7 chord (min7) construction is R–♭3–5–♭7. You can add a minor 7 to a triad by lowering a root one whole step, or raising a 5th by three half steps. Here are some moveable fingerings.

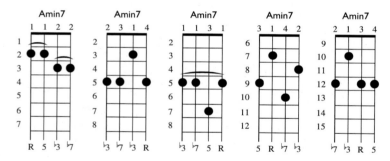

MAJOR 6 CHORDS

A major 6 chord (6) colors a major triad by adding the 6th to the R–3–5. To form a major 6, find a 5th in your chord voicing and raise it one whole step. Below are some moveable fingerings. You may recognize some of these from the minor 7 fingerings. This is because a minor 7 chord has the same notes as a major 6 chord built on a root a minor 3rd higher. For example, an Amin7 has the same notes (A–C–E–G) as a C6 (C–E–G–A).

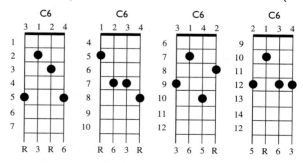

Now try a more colorful version of "Swing By Your Thumbs" using some of the chords you have just learned, plus some new variations. One new trick is the use of *anticipation* in the 7th measure. The C6 from measure 8 is anticipated, or played a half-beat early (on the "&" of beat 4, bar 7). You should also try finding different voicings for these chords using the fingerings on page 82. In this case, play the repeat and the D.C. al Fine!

SWING BY YOUR THUMBS (COOL SWING CHORDS)

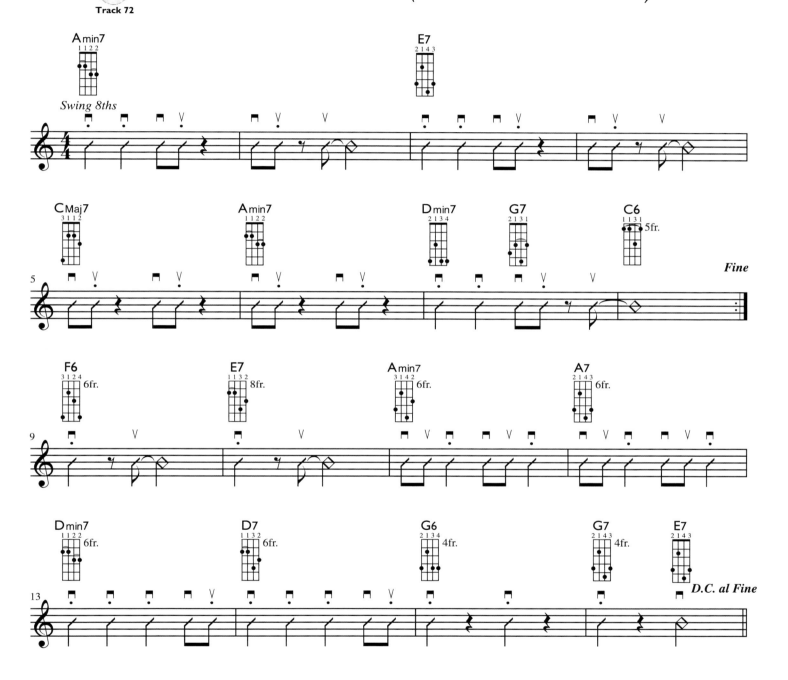

Mastering jazz improvisation can be a life's work, but having fun with it can start right away. As the melodies, rhythms and chords become more developed, the possibilities for what you can do with them widens. Each progression offers new implications for scales, while each melody can be harmonized many ways. Still, jazz improvisation has some of the same roots as blues and bluegrass. Solos can range from slight variations of the melody to advanced, extended explorations of uncharted territory. The chord progression of "Swing By Your Thumbs" offers several opportunities to try new scales and techniques.

"SWING BY YOUR THUMBS" A SECTION—CHANGING SCALES:

The first line of the A section of "Swing By Your Thumbs" is in the key of A Minor. The Amin7 chord fits the natural minor scale (page 64). However, the E7 chord conflicts with this scale. The A Natural Minor scale (shown below) has a G♮ in it. The E7 chord contains a G♯. In order to accommodate the E7 chord, you could use a new scale called the *harmonic minor*. The harmonic minor scale is based on the natural minor scale but raises the minor 7 (♭7, or G) back up to a major 7 (7, or G♯). Here are both scales for you to compare.

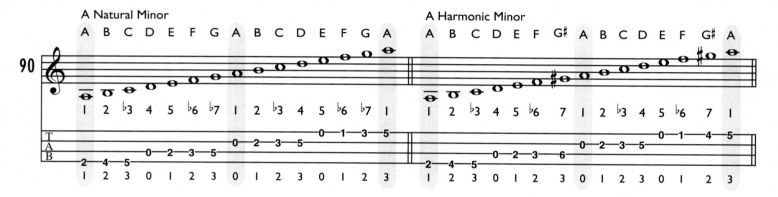

You could use the A Natural Minor scale on the Amin7 chord, then the A Harmonic Minor scale on the E7. The second line of the A section is in C Major (page 8), the relative major (page 64) of A Minor.

"SWING BY YOUR THUMBS" B SECTION: ARPEGGIOS

The B section of the tune changes chords quickly and moves through several possible keys. One easy way to deal with this improvisationally is to play arpeggios of the chords. You can use simple triad arpeggios (pages 60–61) or outline the 6th and 7th chords.

Here is a melody, or "head" for "Swing By Your Thumbs." In the A section, it uses the A Natural Minor scale, the A Harmonic Minor scale and the C Major scale. In the B section, it uses arpeggios of the many chords, with a short melodic run at the end. Don't forget to repeat the A section! On the CD included with this book, you will hear the melody, then a repeat of the chord progression for you to practice your own variations and solos.

SWING BY YOUR THUMBS (MELODY)

Track 73

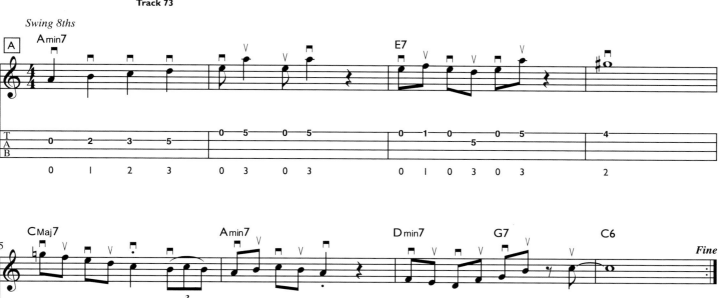

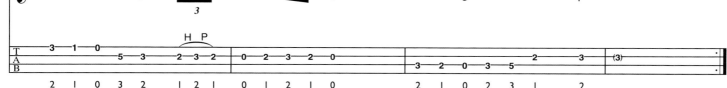

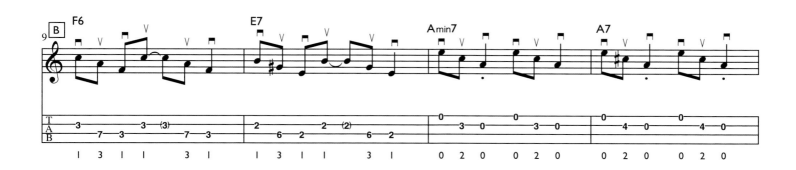

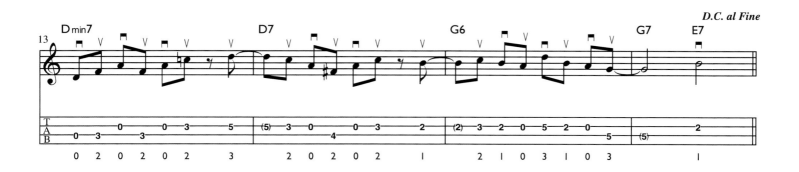

CHAPTER 9

New Rhythms and Sounds

LESSON 1: FUNK ON THE MANDOLIN

Funk music, pioneered by electric artists like Sly and the Family Stone, the Meters, James Brown and George Clinton, uses every instrument in the band like a drum. Layers of rhythm are built up from simple, repeated, interlocking patterns. The mandolin makes a great funk rhythm instrument. Its tight, percussive chop and high pitch makes it sit perfectly in a groove.

SIXTEENTH-NOTE STRUMMING

The foundation of funk strumming technique is sixteenth notes. As you know, there are four sixteenth notes in each beat, counted "1–e–&–ah, 2–e–&–ah" and so on. Try this counting, strumming and foot tapping exercise.

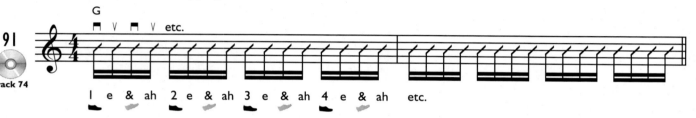

LEFT-HAND MUTING ("SQUEEZING AND SCRATCHING")

The secret of funk strumming is to keep the right hand moving in a steady, down-up sixteenth-note rhythm while the left hand controls the rhythmic accents of the chords. The left hand presses down to sound the chord ("squeeze") and releases the pressure just enough to create a muted, scratching sound. Make sure you don't lift your fingers all the way off the strings. This works best with moveable chord forms that use no open strings.

First, make the A7 chord shown. Then practice "scratching" (indicated by an ✕ instead of a notehead ● or a rhythm slash ╱). Try to set the pressure of your left hand so that no open strings or notes are sounding at all, just the scratch.

✕ = Mute or scratch

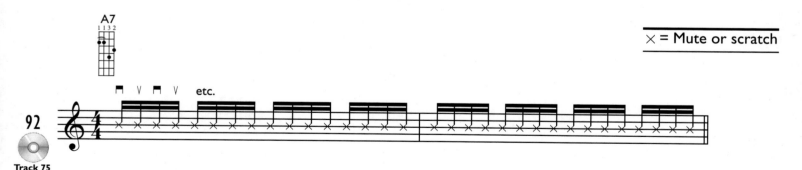

Now try "squeezing" the chord on the first sixteenth of each beat (shown with a slash ╱), relaxing for the other sixteenths. Use the same A7 fingering shown above.

In the following rhythm, squeeze the first two sixteenths and scratch the second two. In the second bar, reverse the pattern.

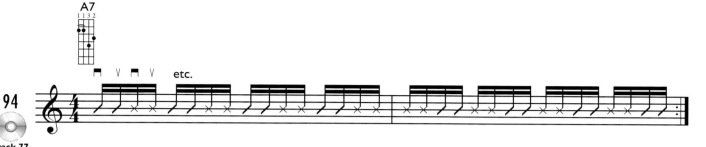

94
Track 77

Try this funk-blues progression. You may want to practice it first with the simpler strums in examples 92–94, then try the funk groove shown. Keep your hand moving in a steady rhythm. Notice that in the first beat of every bar, you will strum a dotted eighth/sixteenth rhythm. Strum down on beat 1, hold the chord through "e-&" and strum up on "ah."

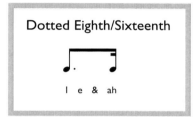

Dotted Eighth/Sixteenth

1   e   &   ah

Remember, a dot increases a note's value by half. Since an eighth note is equal to two sixteenth notes, half of its value is one sixteenth note. Therefore, a dotted eighth note is equal to three sixteenth notes ("1–e–&").

 OOH, THAT SOME FUNKY MANDO!

Track 78

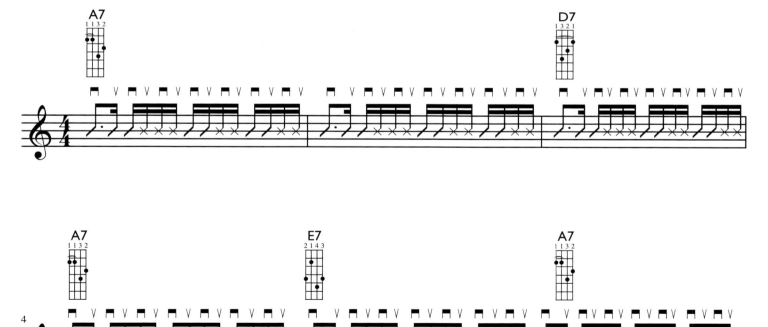

CROSS RHYTHMS AND THE NEW ORLEANS INFLUENCE

In an earlier lesson on ragtime playing (page 36), you learned how to accent eighth notes in groups of three within a simple meter. This sound, sometimes called a *cross rhythm*, is fundamental in rock, funk and blues music. The music of New Orleans, from the earliest "Dixieland" jazz through modern funk and Zydeco, rests on the foundation of simple meter (such as cut time ¢ or $\frac{4}{4}$) with eighth notes grouped in threes.

CLAP THE CLAVE

The *clave* (pronounced KLAH-vay) is an important percussion rhythm born out of the influence of African traditions in the Caribbean, Central and South America. The clave rhythm is traditionally played on wooden sticks called—believe it or not—claves. This rhythm and many variations of it are found in the rhythms of New Orleans jazz and funk. This example shows the clave as a two-bar rhythm in cut time. Remember that in cut time, your foot only taps on beats 1 and 3!

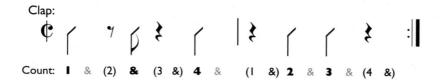

PLAY THE CLAVE

Try strumming the clave rhythm using the "squeezing and scratching" technique you learned on page 86.

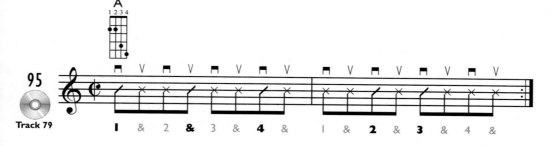

THE BO DIDDLEY BEAT

This is a variation of the clave rhythm made famous by guitarist Bo Diddley. It has been borrowed by Buddy Holly, the Rolling Stones, the Grateful Dead and countless others. David Grisman used it to occasionally break up the bluegrass backbeat of Old and In the Way's "Midnight Moonlight." It looks harder on paper than it is. If you're having trouble, break it down one or two beats at a time.

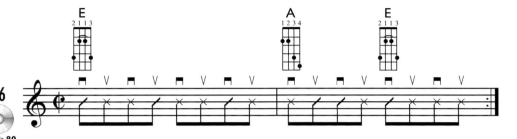

Here is a 12-bar blues in E built on the Bo Diddley beat. Watch out for the simpler bluegrass groove in the third line!

BO MAN DIDDLEY BLUES

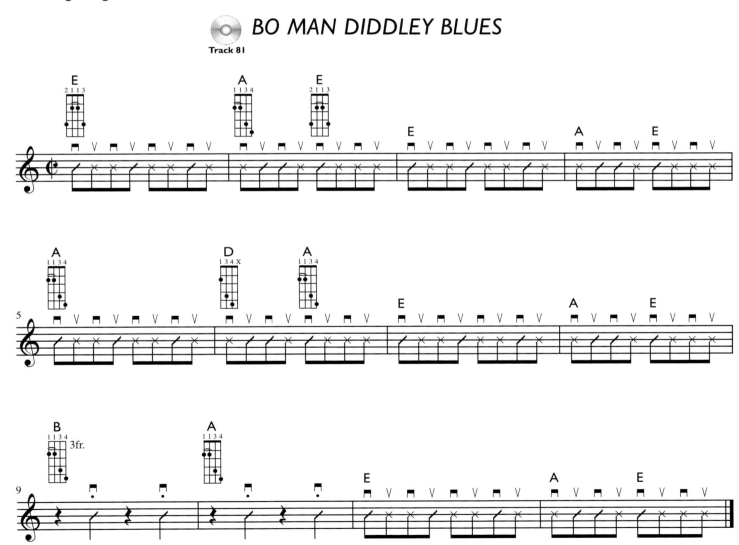

Reggae is the politically charged, infectiously danceable pop music of Jamaica. It combines Caribbean rhythms with the influence of classic American soul music. Modern mandolin pioneer Sam Bush brought the influence of reggae to the mandolin in his solo work and with his band, Newgrass Revival. Bush's rhythm playing was deeply influenced by the guitar techniques of reggae master Bob Marley.

REGGAE STRUMMING

The Reggae Backbeat

Like bluegrass, reggae's foundation is on the backbeat (beats 2 and 4 of a $\frac{4}{4}$ measure). The pace is generally more relaxed in reggae, and the strum often includes the upstroke on the "&" of the beat. Try this pattern using a swing eighth groove.

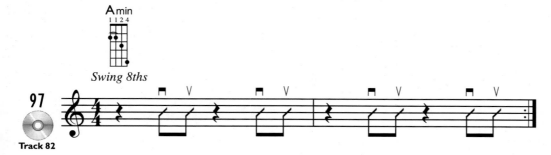

The Bob Marley Backbeat

Bob Marley's guitar technique was marked by clipped, percussive strums that sounded more like a percussion instrument than a chord instrument. He did it by using a variation of the funk squeezing and scratching technique you learned on page 86. Marley would often finger chords, but not quite squeeze them down all the way, just pulsing his fingers on the strings. These finger pulses are marked in this example using staccato eighth notes.

Adding Triplet Fills

When you have the basic groove going, you can vary the groove by adding "scratched" triplets during the rests in the bar. Example 99 adds a triplet on the first beat of bar 1 and the third beat of bar 2.

99

Track 84

Reggae Arpeggios

Here is a reggae-style tune using the rhythms you have learned. The second part of the tune uses reggae-style arpeggios. These often place a rest on the first beat, causing the arpeggio to sound more syncopated and spacious.

HOW A'YOU GONNA PLAY DAT MANDO-LEEN?

Track 85

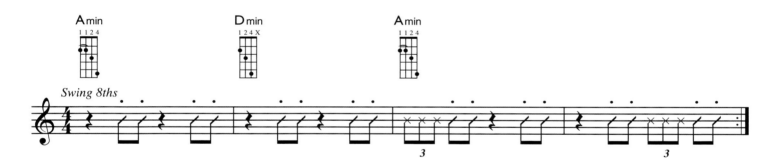

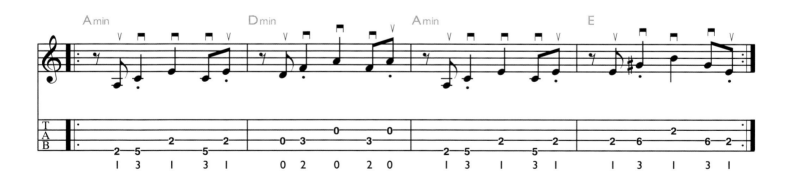

CHAPTER 10

A Taste of Brazil

The music of Brazil has had a huge influence on modern mandolin playing through players such as David Grisman and Mike Marshall. The chief influence comes from the Brazilian musical tradition called *choro*. Choro has its roots in the late 1800s, similar to American ragtime music and it has gone through many declines and revivals since then. It is played by small ensembles featuring string instruments, percussion and wind instruments and is known for unpredictable, leaping melodies, adventurous chord progressions and extremely virtuosic improvisation.

One of the great masters of choro was Jacob do Bandolim (the stage name of Jacob Pick Bittencourt). He was a terrific player of the Portuguese mandolin, called a *bandolim*. Jacob's recordings from the 1950s and '60s are still sought after as wonderful examples of the joy, passion and emotion of choro mandolin. The bandolim is usually teardrop shaped (like an A-style mandolin, but a bit bigger) with a flat or slightly arched top, a round soundhole and a deeper body than American mandolins.

LESSON 1: BRAZILIAN-STYLE RHYTHM PLAYING

In traditional choro music, the following rhythms are played by the *cavaquinho*, the Portuguese ancestor of the ukelele. The bandolim (mandolin) is considered a lead melody instrument. You can get some of the sound of the cavaquinho by learning the strum rhythms shown below. The rhythms in this lesson are drawn from rhythms heard in recordings by Jacob do Bandolim.

Brazilian rhythms are very highly syncopated, and carry the influence of the clave rhythm you learned on page 88. Here is a strum pattern in cut time based on a variation of the clave.

BRAZILIAN STRUM RHYTHM NO. 1—CLAVE VARIATION (SON CLAVE, 3–2)

Below is another common, yet extremely syncopated rhythm. Try tapping all four beats of each bar for a while before trying it in cut time. This one's a whole lot of fun, but you have to work to keep track of the beat!

BRAZILIAN STRUM RHYTHM NO. 2

Here is a chord progression for a tune written in the style of Jacob do Bandolim. It is set in a two-part form (like a fiddle tune) with repeated A and B parts, and includes a new strumming rhythm in the A part.

MANDOLIN JAKE (CHORDS AND RHYTHM)

Track 88

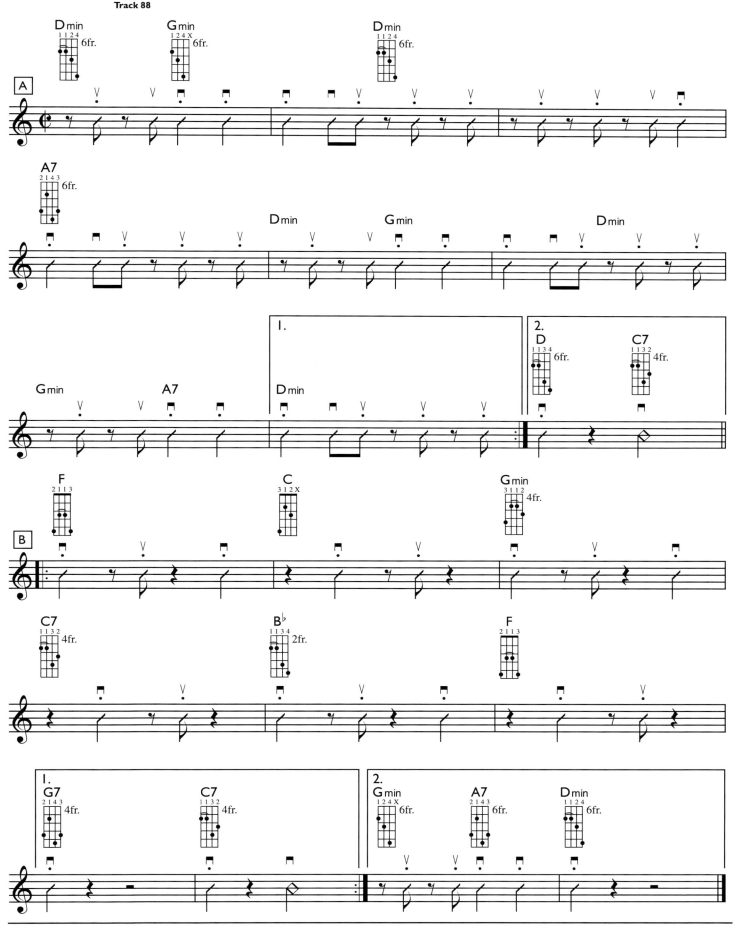

While choro music includes a great deal of improvisation and soloing, the main melodies are so sophisticated that they almost sound like improvised solos themselves. The tunes are full of 7th chord arpeggios, wide melodic leaps, sudden key and scale changes and syncopation.

THE IMPORTANCE OF "TOUCH"

One form of improvisation that is rarely discussed is the improvisational varying of touch. "Touch" refers to the way you articulate a note: You can use a downstroke, upstroke, accent it, play it legato (smooth and connected to other notes) or staccato (clipped and separated from other notes). Touch also includes slides, hammer-ons, pull-offs and any other form of articulation you can think of. Jacob do Bandolim was a master of the subtleties of touch. He would change the way he articulated a melody each time he played it.

Here is the first phrase of the melody of "Mandolin Jake" (page 95) shown with two additional variations based on changing the touch used.

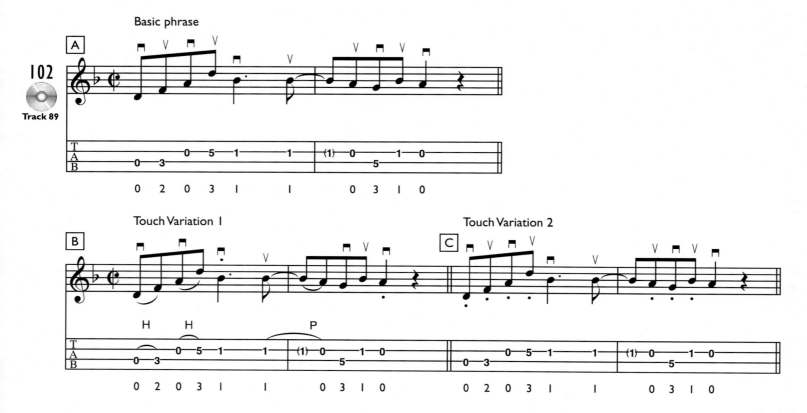

On page 95 is the full melody of "Mandolin Jake." It is full of arpeggios, syncopation, and *chromatic passing tones* (notes outside of the scale that connect notes in the scale, generally in half steps). Specific touch markings have not been indicated; choose your own articulations as you master the tune.

MANDOLIN JAKE (MELODY)

Track 90

Congratulations! You have completed *Intermediate Mandolin*! You've accomplished much.
Don't stop now. We'll see you in *Mastering Mandolin*!